Therefore, my beloved brethren, be ye stedfast, unmoveable, always abounding in the work of the Lord, forasmuch as ye know that your labour is not in vain in the Lord (I Corinthians 15:58).

Maximize Your Day... GOD'S Way

Making Every Day Count

by Marilyn Hickey

Marilyn Hickey Ministries

P.O. Box 17340 • Denver, Colorado 80217

Maximize Your Day . . .
GOD'S Way

Making Every Day Count

CONTENTS

Chapter One

TIME IS THE FRAMEWORK OF OUR LIVES

Have you ever felt that time was slipping through your fingers like grains of sand in an hourglass? I'm sure we all experience such feelings. How often we observe that time has a way of escaping us. There is no doubt about the fact that time, by its very nature, is a transitory dimension; and the time that is ours at this very moment will soon be a part of yesterday. No wonder historians use the expression, "the sands of time," when writing about the passage of events on the pages of human history.

But what is time? It is a measure of existence or the passing of events that irreversibly proceeds from the past, to the present, and on into the future. We date time backwards and forwards, and it can be as long as an eon or as brief as a second. Time can be divided into seconds, minutes, hours, and days. Days become months and years, but actually time is only the moment we have right now.

Although time can be measured, it can't be stored. You may "capture" a moment on film for your photo album, you can "keep" time to the beat of music, or you may "save" time by not wasting it; but there is no way to store time in order to use it for some other occasion. When this moment is gone, it is gone forever.

You can plan for the future and hold memories of the past, but "now" is all the time any of us possess. Therefore, what you do now is of the utmost importance. Don't "while" away your time and say, "In a little while I will do the things I ought to do—or the things I want to do." If you do, time will pass you by; and you will accomplish nothing with your life.

Have you ever wasted a whole day? How did you feel? Most of us feel lousy and depressed after a day in which nothing has been accomplished. We feel that we have been cheated out of something very precious. I believe God made us that way. God has put in all of us a tremendous desire to achieve—in our hearts, our minds, and our emotions. Our days are extremely valuable and certainly not a commodity to be wasted. Just think of it; our lives are measured out to us in units of time.

There are 1,440 opportunities every day to succeed. That is how many minutes there are in each day. I find that putting God first in my day enables me to use my time wisely and accomplish the goals that I have set. It is He Who gives me the wisdom to plan my day, the intelligence to carry out each task, and the energy to do it. And then He gives me the joy and satisfaction of achievement.

What pleasure there is in getting maximum benefit from the minutes and hours which the Lord has given. The Bible speaks about this kind of satisfaction. Proverbs 13:19 says, *"The desire accomplished is sweet to the soul: . . . ."* It is my desire

8

to help you have that kind of sweetness. I want you to maximize your day—God's way.

So far, I have defined time and mentioned the importance of time; but has time always existed? No, God is the Author of time. God, Who is an eternal being without beginning or end, exists outside the dimension of time. Yet He created time and used it as the framework upon which He created the world. Genesis gives us the account of God separating the light from the darkness, thus establishing day and night. In six days God accomplished the monumental work of creation, and on the seventh day He rested:

> *And God called the light Day, and the darkness he called Night. And the evening and the morning were the first day* (Genesis 1:5).
>
> *And God saw every thing that he had made, and, behold, it was very good . . . Thus the heavens and the earth were finished, and all the host of them. And on the seventh day God ended his work which he had made; and he rested on the seventh day from all his work which he had made* (Genesis 1:31; 2:1,2).

Our God could have stepped outside the limitations of time and accomplished His work of creation in some unmeasured dimension. But He did not. I believe God has shown us that all we need to achieve can be achieved in the measure of time we have. God gave Himself 24 hours in each day, no more than He has given to each one of us. God did not fail in achieving His goals; and He does not want us, who are created in His image, to fail in achieving our goals. God has given us enough time.

Because God set time in motion and placed mankind in this realm, I know that time is a gift and not a curse. Even though our lives are passing with the passing of time, we are to rule over our time: it is not to rule over us. But that is easier said than done. We all need to learn how to maximize each day God's way and get the most out of every day He has given to us.

Solomon, the preacher of Ecclesiastes, states that there is a time for everything in the life of any individual. In the first eight verses of Ecclesiastes 3, Solomon gives a brief review of many of life's important things for which there is a time:

> *To every thing there is a season, and a time*
> *to every purpose under the heaven: A time*
> *to be born, and a time to die; . . .*
> (Ecclesiastes 3:1,2).

We realize from the first chapters of Genesis that this earth was created for mankind; and in His infinite wisdom, God chose to place man here in the boundaries and limits of time. As a result, time is the framework upon which we build our lives, just as it was the framework upon which He brought this present world into existence. Time has been the framework for all God has done in the affairs of mankind from the very beginning until now.

In the Lord's relationship with people, He has

always worked in the dimension of time. Although God continually lives outside this confinement and is able to work in unlimited supernatural ways in our behalf, whatever He does must be translated into our existence in order for it to be relevant and effective. Therefore, our heavenly Father has an accepted time for all that He does:

(For he saith, I have heard thee in a time accepted, and in the day of salvation have I succoured thee: . . .) (II Corinthians 6:2).

God took time into account even when planning the means of our eternal salvation. The Word tells us that in the fullness of time God sent His Son. When the Father, Son, and Holy Spirit planned our redemption, it was carefully thought out. Not only was the way in which it would be done of the utmost importance but also the timing. God didn't walk over to the edge of heaven one day and decide it was time to send Jesus into the world. That event was carefully timed so that it would occur at the perfect moment for the greatest benefit:

But when the fulness of the time was come, God sent forth his Son, made of a woman, made under the law, To redeem them that were under the law, that we might receive the adoption of sons (Galatians 4:4,5).

If God seemingly could ignore time which was of His creation but chooses to work everything on our behalf in the framework of time, how important then our time should be to us. Remember, our lives are measured in minutes and days and years. If we are to be successful in life as God desires that we be, then every moment must count. The Word says it is the sluggard who wastes time.

WISE PEOPLE MAKE WISE USE OF TIME

Time is so important; we can see its "footprints" on virtually every page of the Bible from Genesis to the end of Revelation. The last pages of the book of Revelation tell us that at the point when we all step into eternity, time will be no more. But until that last day, it is God's desire for His people to build wisely upon the framework He has given to us.

What we do with time will determine our success or defeat; what we do with time will determine our work and our reward—not only now but also in God's eternal kingdom. God wants His people to be achievers, and that is within the grasp of every one of us through the wise use of our time.

In the Scriptures we read of a man who certainly learned how to maximize his day—God's way. This man's name was Joshua. Joshua was the man whom the Lord chose to lead the people of Israel into Canaan after the death of Moses. Joshua, you will remember, is one of the twelve men sent by Moses to spy out the land of promise. Only Caleb and Joshua came back with a good report—a report of faith. Because Joshua was a man of faith and courage, he was God's choice to go into Canaan and take possession of the land.

Jericho had fallen to Israel under Joshua's leadership and so had Ai. The frightened people of the great city of Gibeon had tricked Israel into making an alliance with them rather than be destroyed. This news was very disturbing to the five kings of the Amorites, so they decided to wage war on the Gibeonites. These kings had no intention of being Israel's next conquest—but God had other plans.

The Gibeonites called upon Israel for help, and Joshua wasted no time in coming to the aid of these people who had become Israel's servants. Joshua and Israel's mighty men of valor fought against the Amorite kings and their armies all in one day. The battle was in Israel's favor, but the day was coming to a close. Joshua knew that to stop the battle was to give an advantage to his adversary, so he cried to the Lord for help.

Joshua gave a startling command that only someone who trusted the Lord and believed in His miraculous help would dare to make: "... *Sun, stand thou still upon Gibeon: and thou, Moon, in the valley of Ajalon"* (Joshua 10:12). Joshua actually asked God to lengthen the day for him so he could finish the battle, and God did exactly that: *"And the sun stood still, and the moon stayed, until the people had avenged themselves upon their enemies . . .* (Joshua 10:13). That is getting the most out of your day.

You see, when you have done your best, you can

even ask for God's miraculous help. I have seen the Lord supernaturally add minutes to my day by enabling me to get more done than I could possibly do under normal circumstances. Sometimes the Lord gives me ideas and shortcuts that save a great deal of my valuable time. Then I feel a little like Joshua when God lengthened his day.

Sometimes it seems God's creatures have more wisdom when it comes to using time wisely than His children do. The Lord put guidance systems into the members of the animal kingdom, which we call instinct; and even the tiniest creatures know how to manage their time in a beneficial way. Their very existence depends upon what they do with their time. The Word of God gives us several illustrations of this, and He tells us we should consider their ways:

> *Go to the ant, . . . consider her ways, and be wise: Which having no guide, overseer, or ruler, Provideth her meat in the summer, and gathereth her food in the harvest* (Proverbs 6:6-8).

> *There be four things which are little upon the earth, but they are exceeding wise: The ants are a people not strong, yet they prepare their meat in the summer: The conies are but a feeble folk, yet make they their houses in the rocks; The locusts have no king, yet go they forth all of them by bands; The spider taketh hold with her hands, and is in kings' palaces* (Proverbs 30:24-28).

Those of us in the human family have been given the gift of free will, which means that we have the ability to choose our pattern of behavior. We can't depend on doing most things by instinct like the rest of God's creatures. We have to be trained, taught, and disciplined to order our time and our behavior so that we derive the most benefit from the time the Lord has given to us.

As a matter of fact if left to its own devices, humanity will generally do things wrong rather than do them right. That is the old sin nature at work. People who have no direction will waste their time and achieve nothing with their lives:

> *How long wilt thou sleep, O sluggard? when wilt thou arise out of thy sleep? Yet a little sleep, a little slumber, a little folding of the hands to sleep: So shall thy poverty come as one that travelleth, and thy want as an armed man* (Proverbs 6:9-11).

No wonder the admonition of God's Word is: *"So teach us to number our days, that we may apply our hearts unto wisdom"* (Psalms 90:12). I believe the Lord is telling us how important it is to carefully plan each and every day so we may be achievers. Success is accomplished one day at a time, and there is no time like the present. The Lord tells us that "now is the accepted time" to get things done. We have no moment but now:

> *(. . . behold, now is the accepted time; behold, now is the day of salvation)* (II Corinthians 6:2).

In examining the earthly life of the Lord Jesus, we see that time was very important to Him. In Jesus' earthly ministry, He never stepped out of time or His humanity to perform the supernatural. This is precisely what Satan intended when he tempted Jesus at the very beginning of His ministry. But Jesus refused the temptation with the Word of God. Jesus knew that all His needs would be met at the right time. In this instance, the Word tells us that after Satan left Jesus, angels came to care for Him. Jesus always depended upon the Father's timing:

> *Then the devil leaveth him, and, behold, angels came and ministered unto him* (Matthew 4:11).

Let's take a closer look at this particular situation. Jesus had spent 40 days alone with the Father. I believe Jesus' full attention was given to the Father's instructions concerning Jesus' ministry during the very short time He would have to complete His work on earth. He was more interested in hearing the Father's voice than in sustaining His body with food. Jesus continually rested in the fact that events in His life would never be too early or too late while obeying the Father's guidance.

However, the devil knew that Jesus had to be hungry—at the point of starvation. Satan considered this to be a weak moment for our Lord, and he was determined to take advantage of the situation. Satan tempted Jesus with food, fame, and power: a temptation that was aimed at Jesus' spirit, soul, and body. It was targeted at future goals as well as immediate needs.

The devil wanted Jesus to get God's plan completely off schedule and out of order so Jesus would fail in the work of redemption. But Jesus knew there was a right time and a right way. Our Lord had the patience and confidence to trust God's order, and He would not ruin the plan by taking up His divine nature to get His way even when it meant going to the cross:

> *And he* [Jesus] *went a little farther, and fell on his face, and prayed, saying, O my Father, if it be possible, let this cup pass from me: nevertheless not as I will, but as thou wilt* (Matthew 26:39).

Jesus was all man, and He placed the same time limitations on Himself that we have; but what profound use He made of the time which was allotted to Him! Jesus never wasted time; yet He never cut corners. Time was always a consideration in everything Jesus did. From the very beginning of Christ's ministry, we see that He was always conscious of what time it was in regard to the work He had come to do.

At a marriage feast in the city of Cana near his hometown of Nazareth, Jesus performed His first miracle by turning water into the additional wine needed for the feast. Although Jesus responded to the request of His mother, it appears Mary may have wanted her Son to reveal Himself as the Messiah at that time. Nevertheless, He said: " . . . *mine hour is not yet come*" (John 2:4).

Once when traveling northward into Galilee, Jesus told his disciples that He had to go through Samaria. Although most Jews avoided such a route, Jesus deliberately went that way to keep a divine appointment with a woman whom even the detestable Samaritans avoided because of her immoral lifestyle. Our Lord knew by the Spirit the precise moment this woman would come to Jacob's well to draw water, and He planned to be there to offer her "the water of Life."

Although the townsfolk judged this woman by her actions, Jesus looked at her heart and saw a person who would receive Him as her Savior and Lord. He knew there would be no other time nor place when He could touch this woman's life. If Jesus had missed this moment, He would have forfeited the opportunity to impact her life and the lives of everyone in that Samaritan town. (See John 4:3-42.)

> . . . *for the LORD seeth not as man seeth; for man looketh on the outward appearance, but the LORD looketh on the heart* (I Samuel 16:7).

In another instance when word reached Jesus that his dear friend Lazarus was gravely ill, the Lord purposely waited four days before going to Bethany, the place where Lazarus lay so ill. Of course, Jesus knew that his sick friend would now be dead. What looked like lack of concern and bad timing were really the elements for a greater miracle than healing, because Jesus then raised Lazarus from the dead. His purpose and timing were in complete harmony.

What was Christ's attitude about the time given to Him as a man? Hear what Jesus Himself had to say about the value and use of His time. Realizing that precious moments would soon be gone forever, Jesus said: *"I must work the works of him that sent me, while it is day: the night cometh, when no man can work"* (John 9:4).

TIME IS OF GREAT VALUE

It is obvious from these illustrations and Jesus' own words that Jesus viewed time as very valuable. Every moment contained the potential for touching precious lives. With the guidance of the Holy Spirit, Jesus used wisely the time He knew was allotted to Him. Jesus made every moment of every day count in doing those things for which He had come to earth, but a part of every day was spent in fellowship with His heavenly Father.

How about you? Have you ever been tempted to do things your way, to ignore time with the Lord or the instruction of His Word? Have you ignored the instruction of your boss or even the directions that came with a new gadget? I'm sure we have all "cut corners" or omitted things in order to "save" time. But you didn't save time, you actually wasted it.

I remind God and myself that He is a rewarder of them that diligently seek Him. When I set aside a time

19

daily to seek Him, I know that God is going to reward me for that time I spend with Him. Diligence brings reward; lack of diligence brings no reward. If you are faithful in praying and set aside a special time of day for prayer, then He will reward you for spending time in His presence and you will find that somehow your time is multiplied. Omit this time with the Lord, and the time you hoped to save will be lost in some way.

Have you ever lost sight of your goals for some immediate gratification? This also is a waste of time. The wise use of time will put order into your day and will successfully define your future. People who are successful in life are those people who have not squandered away their lives one day at a time. They are people who have taken every hour and every day into account; they make wise use of their time. If you do not plan to accomplish certain things each day, your life and future will be simply an accident ruled by circumstance.

God's Word tells us that a wise individual redeems the time because the days are evil. The word *redeem* means "to buy up" or "to rescue from loss." In other words if you do not work toward making your moments count for some purpose or accomplishment, you have lost that time—lost it forever. If you are not conducting the affairs of your days in a wise and orderly fashion, you are succumbing to the effects and influences of the world's evil order:

> *See then that ye walk circumspectly, not as fools, but as wise, Redeeming the time,*

20

because the days are evil (Ephesians 5:15,16).

I spend many hours on planes as I travel back and forth to various meetings. During this time I always plan to read my Bible and study. Nevertheless, I'm also looking for opportunities to share the Lord Jesus with others. Once, because I boarded my plane a bit late, I had to climb over the man sitting on the aisle to get to my seat. He had already put his belongings, not only under his seat, but under mine too. He refused to move these items, so I had to hold my briefcase.

I began to look over my sermon notes while the man ordered one drink after another. I was so "turned off" by this man, and I certainly wasn't in the mood to talk to him. When he finally spoke to me, he said, "Are you reading a Bible?" You can imagine how surprised I was that this man should ask such a question.

I replied curtly, "Yes, I am." Then he asked, "Could you answer a question?" He told me that he had been born again one week earlier. Since then someone had told him about the baptism of the Holy Spirit, and he wanted to know if I knew anything about the experience. Silently I repented, then I began ministering the Word to that man. How thankful I was that I had been privileged to "buy up" that precious time.

Once there was a wise king in Judah who knew how to redeem the time in an evil day. This man, whose name was Hezekiah, was a very godly king.

He had taken down the idols and reestablished the Passover and other feast days along with Temple worship and sacrifices. Nevertheless, good king Hezekiah ran into trouble.

Sennacherib, the king of Assyria, marched into Judah after invading Israel and camped against the walled cities. Hezekiah knew that Sennacherib intended to attack the capital city of Jerusalem. The king was afraid, but he was wise enough to turn to God. Hezekiah didn't sit around crying and wringing his hands while waiting for the attack. I call him a godly opportunist.

Hezekiah wasted no time in gathering together the princes and the mighty men to formulate a plan. Together with many willing people they "stopped" the brooks and fountains outside the city walls. This group managed to channel all the water into the city by cutting a lengthy tunnel through solid rock. Thus the inhabitants of Jerusalem were supplied with much-needed water while the enemy was deprived of this precious commodity.

Not only did Hezekiah and his people do what they could do with the time they had but the king and the prophet Isaiah prayed earnestly to the Lord for Judah's deliverance. Then the Lord sent an angel into the enemy camp to slay all the mighty men of Assyria. Stripped of his best warriors Sennacherib went home in shame and defeat.

Hezekiah's water course still exists today as a memorial to a wise man who made the most of his

God-given time. Do you know how I know that? I know because I have waded through that quarter mile of tunnel where water still flows into Jerusalem and empties into the pool of Siloam. (If you want to read this story about Hezekiah, it can be found in II Chronicles 32:1-23.)

MAKE YOUR MOMENTS COUNT

Have you noticed there is no way you can go back and redeem yesterday's lost opportunities or do the things that needed to be done then? Not only did you lose yesterday, but you are behind today. Unfortunately, while certain opportunities are gone forever, all those things that could have and should have been done yesterday do not vanish as does the day; but they are all there to be done today. This will inevitably put stress and confusion into your life.

There is an old adage that says, "Never put off until tomorrow what can be done today." Perhaps you and I have laughed when we heard someone turn this around to say, "Never do today what can be put off until tomorrow." It really isn't funny at all, but we all probably have identified with the results of such behavior.

I will never forget an uncle of Wally's. Day after day the gentleman would sit on his front porch and rock back and forth in his rocker and say, "I wish I had a million dollars, I wish I had a million dollars." Do you think this man ever got his million dollars? Of course not! Although he had a wish, it never materialized because he never put any time or effort into the project of getting a million dollars. He was content just to sit and rock on his porch while a million moments of opportunity passed him by.

Recently I read a statement that impressed me. It said, "Self-discipline is the yoke of a free person." One doesn't normally think of a yoke being synonymous with freedom. However, in my mind's eye, I saw Jesus standing with outstretched arms calling to everyone:

*Come unto me, all ye that labour and are heavy laden, and I will give you rest. Take my **yoke** upon you, and learn of me; for I am meek and lowly in heart: and ye shall find rest unto your souls. For my **yoke** is easy, and my burden is light* (Matthew 11:28-30).

I know that Jesus was contrasting the works of man-made rules and rituals with simply resting in Jesus for salvation. However, I thought how Jesus would lighten our daily burdens and give us real freedom and rest if we would place upon ourselves the "yoke of discipline" regarding our time. Like Lazarus' sister Martha, we are often burdened about *many* things, when a measure of discipline in our day could restore order and peace to our lives. We need to decide which things are the most important and which things are not. Then we can use our time successfully.

An undisciplined life is a hectic, disorderly, and

confused existence. More time is wasted on trivial and unnecessary things than on those things which really count. There is simply no way to bring peace and order to your day without the willingness to discipline your time. Much more will be said about discipline in another chapter of this book. Nevertheless, I thought it appropriate in this first chapter, which deals with the value and wise use of time, to mention the necessity of putting discipline into the minutes of our day.

Learning to maximize your day—God's way—requires many ingredients. Some of these ingredients are effort, diligence, knowledge, faith—and lots of patience with oneself, others, and the task at hand. If you plan to make wise use of your day, and therefore your life, proper training and skill are often necessary. It goes without saying that you need to know what it is you want to do before planning a course of action. Don't start running without knowing where it is you are going.

Remember, each second, each hour, each day is a gift from God. Begin your day in fellowship with the Lord, and receive direction from Him. Keep Him in the midst of every plan, every action, and every circumstance. In the good times and in the bad times, always maintain a "gratitude attitude." Our God is able to turn the bad days into good days and bring order out of disorder. Life is a precious treasure: how you spend your days here will count for eternity:

This is the day which the Lord hath made; we will rejoice and be glad in it (Psalms 118:24).

25

Chapter Two

CATCH A VISION

WHAT IS A VISION?

"Where there is no vision, the people perish." These words were written many years ago by King Solomon, and they have been recorded for us in the Old Testament book of Proverbs. Adding to his thought, Solomon said, *"but he that keepeth the law, happy is he."* Except for the Lord Jesus, the Bible tells us that King Solomon was the wisest person who ever lived, so I think that we should all pay attention to what he had to say, don't you? Although these words of Solomon's were recorded over 2500 years ago, they are as true today as the day in which they were written:

Where there is no vision, the people perish:
but he that keepeth the law, happy is he
(Proverbs 29:18).

King Solomon received his great wisdom from God when he asked the Lord for the ability to rule the people of Israel wisely. Solomon was already wise enough to know that without God's insights and direction he would fail. Solomon needed a "vision" of how God would have a king rule His people of Israel. Solomon knew that without that vision he and the people would perish, and he put many of his valuable insights into a book of proverbs. Of course, we know that all of Solomon's proverbs were inspired by the Holy Spirit, Who saw to their preservation in the Holy Bible. (See II Timothy 3:16.) Isn't it wonderful that even today we can read and heed His instruction?

You may be asking yourself, "How does having a vision relate to maximizing your day God's way?" First, we need to understand what is meant by the word *vision*. Many people think a vision is something only a prophet has when he goes into a trance and sees things that aren't really there. Indeed, Old Testament "seers" did, and modern-day prophets still do *see* things in the spirit which are given by the Lord, and that is a vision.

However, the kind of vision to which Solomon referred is the ability to contemplate or perceive plans and ideas. The Hebrew word used in Proverbs 29:18 is *chazown* which means "a mental sight" (picture) or "revelation." This word is closely related to *chazah*, meaning "to gaze at," "to perceive mentally," "to contemplate (with pleasure)," and the word even means "to provide." So we see that a *vision* is the provision of plans and ideas pictured in your mind to give you proper direction and to keep you from falling or "perishing." Without a vision of what is to be accomplished, you cannot use time effectively.

Can you imagine the kind of demands that were made on the time of a ruler like Solomon? His days were filled to overflowing with counseling his subjects and guiding the affairs of state. Solomon certainly needed to maximize his day God's way;

therefore, he needed a *vision* or a *plan* so that he could wisely order his time and get the greatest benefit from the minutes and hours of each and every day. And I know he didn't have a "Day-Timer."

Solomon was definitely not unique in needing the ability to plan his day. We live in a time when our lives may be even more demanding than Solomon's. Certainly Solomon didn't have to find time in his busy schedule to arrange a flight to Sheba to see the Queen. She came to him (I Kings 10:1-10). Neither was the telephone "ringing off the wall" while Solomon decided which baby belonged to which mother (I Kings 3:16-28). On the other hand, I'm sure a thousand wives and concubines could be very distracting.

As a matter of fact, Solomon did become so distracted by the women in his life that he lost sight of his vision and the plan God had for his life. Ignoring God's command for the kings not to marry heathen women, Solomon brought them into the palace with all their "baggage," which included many false gods and idols. No longer was his life or his time ordered by the Lord.

Solomon did not keep the vision or *the* Book before his eyes; and therefore, he filled his hours and days with many vain and unprofitable things. Without the vision, Solomon failed—for a while. Although the story has a happy ending, which you can read in the book of Ecclesiastes, it is so unfortunate that Solomon wasted many valuable days and years on worldly pursuits. When all those things became stale and meaningless, Solomon still had the wisdom to turn back to God and his vision:

> *Remember now thy Creator in the days of thy youth, while the evil days come not, or the years draw nigh, when thou shalt say, I have no pleasure in them* (Ecclesiastes 12:1).
>
> *Let us hear the conclusion of the whole matter: Fear God, and keep his commandment: for this is the whole duty of man* (Ecclesiastes 12:13).

CATCH A VISION OF GOD

I want to go back to Proverbs 29:18. The last half of the proverb says, *"but he that keepeth the law, happy is he."* The Lord is telling us through Solomon that we will never catch the right vision for our lives until we know the Word of God. Let me say it this way: we will never have the vision which will bring happiness and success in our lives until we have a vision of God.

The Lord God reveals Himself to us through the Word of God. He wants us all to have a true picture of Who He is and what He is like. You see, we will never have the right concept of God without the Word of God because He is mirrored in its pages. Only with a true vision of God can we have a true vision of ourselves. It is absolutely necessary for each of us to have the right perspective or view of who we are in order to catch the proper vision for our lives.

Those of you who were raised in Sunday school will probably remember a song that went like this: "Zacchaeus was a wee little man, a wee little man was he, he climbed up in a sycamore tree, the Lord he wanted to see . . . ." Composed about an incident in Luke 19:1-9, the song tells of a man who had a *strong* desire to see Jesus. A large crowd of people thronged the streets of Jericho that day also wanting to see Jesus. Since Zacchaeus was very small in stature, he climbed into a tree to make certain he would see this Jesus, of whom so much was being said.

On the outside Zacchaeus had many things against him. The people hated him because he was a tax collector or publican, who had "sold his soul" to the Roman government for illegal gain. All publicans made their living by taxing the Jews more than Rome demanded, and Zacchaeus had required *much* more than necessary. By putting the extra in his pocket, he had become very rich. So you see, Zacchaeus was not the most popular man in town.

Not only was Zacchaeus lacking in social acceptance, he was also lacking in physical stature. Zacchaeus knew there was a chance of being trampled in the crowd that day by people who really wouldn't have cared, but he was *determined* to see Jesus. I wonder what this little man had heard about Jesus—that he was a healer and a miracle worker? Do you suppose Zacchaeus thought Jesus could add a few inches to his height? I don't think so, because of what followed. I believe Zacchaeus had heard the "Son of

31

David'' could forgive sin, and I think Zacchaeus was burdened with a load of sin.

On the *inside* Zacchaeus had everything going for him. Although others may have judged Zacchaeus as having a very "black" heart, Jesus did not. Jesus knew this little man was hungry for a vision of God, hungry for repentance and righteousness. It wasn't the "important" religious men of Jericho Jesus met with that day; it was one small man whom He called down from a tree. Zacchaeus—determined that nothing would get in his way, not the crowd, not his height, not his sin—received a clear vision of the Lord, himself, and a new direction. I don't know what Zacchaeus did after paying back all the illegal gain, but I do know he won the respect of the people and found joy and happiness:

> *O taste and see that the LORD is good:* . . .
> *they that seek the LORD shall not want any*
> *good thing* (Psalms 34:8,10).

What are the things *we* need to know about God to have a true vision of Him? We need to know Who He is; we need an insight into His personality. We need to know His nature and His attributes, and we also need to be acquainted with His character. This combination of God's qualities has determined all His plans and activities both in the past and the present, as well as in the future. When we have an understanding of God, we understand better why He does the things He does.

Unfortunately, many people tend to view the Lord's

commandments, statutes, and laws as the harsh rules of a rigid God which need to be obeyed—or else. Actually they are all gracious instructions from a loving Father Who wants to guide and protect each moment in every day of our lives. More than that, they are a revelation of Who God is. God is love—kind, just, merciful, gracious, quick to hear, not willing that any should perish. He is peace, joy, truth, life, and so very much more. To know Him is to love Him, and to love Him is to obey Him:

We love Him, because He first loved us
(I John 4:19).

Pages have been written on the person and character of God, but that is not my purpose here. I want *you* to dig into the Word daily and invite the Holy Spirit to reveal the Lord to you in an ever-increasing way. Nevertheless, I am going to mention some very important aspects of God in these pages to establish the basis on which you can receive a vision of God which applies to our subject of maximizing your day God's way.

God is a divine, eternal Trinity—Father, Son, and Holy Spirit—Who is all-powerful, all-knowing, and ever-present. God created the universe with His Word, and He is sovereign over all His creation. God's Word is as certain as His very existence: God and His Word are one. Therefore, the Word is established forever as changeless as God Himself. How thankful we should be that the Lord has graciously given us His written Word through which you and I can catch a vision of Him and His promises.

It isn't enough to know what God has done; we need to know how He feels and thinks. Some philosophers believe that, although God or some "higher power" created the world and mankind, He is an impersonal, uncaring entity who is not involved in our affairs. Nothing is further from the truth! The Scriptures tell us that mankind was fashioned for God's pleasure. As sons and daughters, we were made in His image and likeness; and He created the world as our home:

> *And God said, Let us make man in our image, after our likeness: and let them have dominion . . . over all the earth . . .* (Genesis 1:26).
>
> *Thou art worthy, O Lord, to receive glory and honour and power: for thou hast created all things, and for thy pleasure they are and were created* (Revelation 4:11).

You and I know that God didn't leave His family; the family chose to leave the Father through disobedience to His Word. The Lord gave His children, Adam and Eve, dominion and authority over their home; but they forfeited it to the devil—and sin entered the human race, bringing spiritual death, and separating the children from the Father.

But remember, the Father created the children for His pleasure, and He wasn't going to give up *His* vision of *us* that easily. He had a plan, and that plan was His divine Son Jesus. God promised that He would send a Savior, completely divine but completely human, to buy us back with the price of His own shed blood. That tremendous act of love is documented history now, and by simply a choice anyone can be restored into the family of God, with sins forgiven, because Jesus took our sin upon Himself:

For God so loved the world, that he gave his only begotten Son, that whosoever believeth in him should not perish, but have everlasting life (John 3:16).

Jesus' powerful resurrection from the dead proved not only that God had done what He promised, but it also proved beyond any shadow of a doubt how exceedingly He loves each one of us. Almighty God has redeemed and restored His vision. I've mentioned all these things about our wonderful Lord that in catching a greater vision of Him, you may catch the love vision He has of you. Then *you* can catch a supernatural, God-given vision of yourself. And with that vision of yourself, I want you to be inspired to envision and accomplish great things with your life:

Greater love hath no man than this, that a man lay down his life for his friends (John 15:13).

CATCH GOD'S VISION OF YOU

How does God see His children? He sees them in Jesus Christ. The apostle Paul received the greatest "vision" or revelation of who we are in Christ than any other writer of the Scriptures. God gave that revelation to Paul so that we may know just how the Lord sees us and how we should see ourselves. It is very important for you to know how God sees you, so you can see yourself likewise:

> *Blessed be the God and Father of our Lord Jesus Christ, who hath blessed us with all spiritual blessings in heavenly places in Christ: According as he hath chosen us in him before the foundation of the world, that we should be holy and without blame before him in love: Having predestinated us unto the adoption of children by Jesus Christ to himself, according to the good pleasure of his will, To the praise of the glory of his grace, wherein he hath made us accepted in the beloved. In whom we have redemption through his blood, the forgiveness of sins, according to the riches of his grace: Wherein he hath abounded toward us in all wisdom and prudence; Having made known unto us the mystery of his will, according to his good pleasure . . .* (Ephesians 1:3-9).

But people often have a bad view of themselves. A negative vision doesn't always involve the devil, but he is always willing to assist. Enemies and "friends" may lend a hand. Unrealistic expectations or negative expectations can bring frustration and discouragement, and past defeats and failures often give a dim view of the future. There are always the "prophets of doom and gloom" to discourage us. Unless we see who we are in Christ, we tend to view ourselves as unable, insufficient, and inadequate. But the Lord desires for us to see ourselves as able, sufficient, and adequate—*in* Christ:

> *According as his divine power hath given*
> *unto us all things that pertain unto life and*
> *godliness, through the knowledge of him that*
> *hath called us to glory and virtue: Whereby*
> *are given unto us exceeding great and*
> *precious promises: that by these ye might be*
> *partakers of the divine nature, having*
> *escaped the corruption that is in the world*
> *through lust* (II Peter 1:3,4).

I love to study the lives of people in the Old Testament. The Word tells us these accounts are given to us as examples. One of my favorite people is Gideon, whose story is told in Judges 6, 7, and 8. The Lord had allowed the Midianites to overrun Israel because His people had fallen into idolatry. Finally, the people cried out to God and He heard them. However, God chose what looked like the worst possible solution; he sent an angel to Gideon, who was so frightened and insecure he hid himself at night to thresh a little bit of grain. If ever anyone had a bad self-image, Gideon did. Frankly, I would have chosen someone else.

It gets worse. The angel said to Gideon, *"The LORD is with thee, thou mighty man of valour."* What? This must be a case of mistaken identity! The coward immediately began to complain about God, the circumstances, his family, and himself. Can you believe Gideon means "warrior" or "destroyer"? At least his parents had the right idea.

Gideon was smart enough to know that he was in a heavenly presence when the meal he prepared for the Messenger was not eaten but consumed with fire as a sacrifice. However, that didn't make Gideon feel any better. Now Gideon thought he would die because he had been in the presence of the Lord. But the Lord continued to give Gideon His encouraging words and directions. Little by little God replaced Gideon's negative vision of himself and his purpose with a godly vision.

Under the veil of darkness, Gideon, still fearful, began to act on the word of the Lord. He cut down the heathen grove, tore down his father's altar of Baal, and built an altar to the Lord, upon which he sacrificed one of his father's own bulls. The city folks decided that action was worthy of the death penalty; but Gideon's father convinced the people that if Baal really was a god, he could defend himself. When nothing happened, all Israel supported Gideon. However, it didn't take long for the Midianites to hear the "bad" news and make ready for war.

Still not sure He wanted to be God's *destroyer*, Gideon put out a "fleece" to make certain he had heard from God; but God assured Gideon he was the man. You probably remember how the Lord routed the huge army of the enemy as Gideon and his troops, which the Lord "whittled" down to 300 good men, simply blew trumpets and broke the pitchers which they carried, exposing the lamps inside. Thinking they were encircled by a huge army, the frightened Midianites, " . . . *ran, and cried, and fled*" (Judges 7:21) in the dark, killing each other as they went. Gideon may have thought his life was just an unfortunate accident with no direction or purpose, but God's Word gave Gideon a vision of hope, purpose, and victory.

Neither are you just an accident. God had a vision of **you** as an individual before he framed the world, and you were divinely created for delightful fellowship with Him. Not only that, God has given you a unique personality with specific attributes and talents to put you over in this life. God intends for you to be an overcomer both "here" and "hereafter." He has made an everlasting provision for you, a *provision* for your vision:

> *For we are his workmanship, created in Christ Jesus unto good works, which God hath before ordained that we should walk in them* (Ephesians 2:10).

Let me tell you what the Lord has said about you through the prophet Jeremiah. You can find it in chapter 29, verse 11: *"For I know the thoughts that I think toward you, saith the LORD, thoughts of peace, and not of evil, to give you an expected end."* The New International Version states it this way:

" *'For I know the plans I have for you,' declares the* LORD, *'plans to prosper you and not to harm you, plans to give you hope and a future.'* " Isn't that **good** news?

Oh, I know Jeremiah was speaking about His people Israel at a specific time in history. However, we too are His people by faith; and God is no respecter of persons. What He has done for others, He can do for you. Don't forget that God's Word is as sure today as it was yesterday. The Lord is telling you that He has thought a lot about *you*, and He has designed a plan for your life that will bring ultimate joy and success to you as a person.

Do you believe that God's thoughts are perfect and that His ways are perfect? I do. He has a vision that has been designed and carefully planned exactly for you. Just as there is no one else in the world like you, there is no other person in the world who can carry out that plan. But you say, "What is that plan, and how do I find it?" or "I already have a plan for my life; how do I know if it is God's plan?"

CATCH A VISION FOR YOUR LIFE

Let me tell you of my own personal experience. For a number of years, I had taught Bible studies. Not only was I teaching in the church which my husband, Wally, pastored but I also taught several Bible studies throughout Denver and Colorado. I had even begun traveling some. Although the Lord certainly was

40

blessing in these endeavors, I did not have a clear vision of God's call on my life. I knew my gift was teaching, but I didn't know whether I was called to the ministry as a teacher in the Body of Christ.

Back when I started expanding the Bible studies and teaching in other churches, it wasn't easy for a woman to take a place of leadership in the Church. Although I received gracious invitations from many pastors, I also received a great deal of opposition. One evangelist rebuked me soundly and told me I should be content as a pastor's wife and homemaker. Troubled, I searched the Scriptures for an answer from the Lord because I certainly wanted to be in His divine will. I found in the Bible numerous women who held positions of leadership including Deborah, who was God's prophetess. My heart began to be satisfied that the insatiable desire to teach God's Word was from the Lord!

You know, God is so good. One day when I was in real turmoil about this whole issue, I shared it with a friend. Her practical answer was, ''Have you asked Wally how he feels about this? Wally has always been so supportive of you. Does he feel you are usurping his authority, either as a husband or pastor?'' Why hadn't I thought of that? When I talked it over with Wally, he was more supportive of me than ever. He told me it would be wrong not to use my gift. Wally had no problem with what I was doing, and he encouraged me to do more. Praise the Lord!

In spite of this assurance and an increasing demand

for my teaching, I still wasn't completely certain about the direction God wanted my ministry to take. One day while I was in another city for a teaching seminar, I slipped away to the shore of a lovely lake. There I spent time in prayer and meditation. I asked the Lord just what He wanted me to do. I have to tell you that I was somewhat amazed when He answered very clearly in my heart, "I want you to *cover the earth* with My Word." Not only did God confirm my vision, but He also enlarged it! No longer was there any question about what I was to do or where I was to do it. I had caught God's vision for my life.

The way has not always been easy, and God didn't just "roll out the red carpet" for me. Many times I have not known what was around the next bend in the road until I had turned into it. There have been difficulties of all sorts, but the Lord has worked out all of them. The one sure and certain thing I have is God's vision for my life; it keeps me on course, it gives me joy and fulfillment. But that isn't all, the lives of multitudes of people are being changed and blessed through the Word of God as I allow the Lord to work out His vision for me. I believe with all my heart that when we are living out our vision, others will always be blessed and we may often inspire a vision in someone else.

Perhaps you have a clear vision for your life, and you are experiencing the joy of "walking out" that vision. I pray this will encourage you to stay on course. However, many people who are reading this book are either unsure of their vision or simply haven't yet caught that vision. I want to remind you of the things I did. First, I knew my talents, abilities, and desires. I loved to teach and had received my teaching degree, after which I had taught in public schools. I felt successful when I was teaching.

Let's take an inventory of you. What are the things in which you are most interested? At what do you feel competent, even though you may be just a beginner? What do you imagine yourself doing when you see yourself as you want to see yourself? If you could be anything you desired, what would it be? Tell me what you would be doing if time, money, position, or age were not a consideration.

I want to expand your thinking beyond all those things which you see as limitations. Whether you are 6 or 60 plus, it isn't too late to catch a vision or recapture one which seems to have been lost. Yes, you have to be practical and realistic, but too often people ''pen up'' their vision with a fence of limitations that keeps them from seeing beyond that pen. Free your mind and heart from handicaps; meditate on God and His Word; and see what He shows you. When you get the right perspective, certain aspects of your personality and circumstances can be accepted, not as limitations, but as guidelines:

> *But as it is written, Eye hath not seen, nor ear heard, neither have entered into the heart of man, the things which God hath prepared for them that love him. But God*

hath revealed them unto us by his Spirit:. . .
(I Corinthians 2:9,10).
*That the God of our Lord Jesus Christ, the
Father of glory, may give unto you the spirit
of wisdom and revelation in the knowledge
of him: The eyes of your understanding
being enlightened: that ye may know what
is the hope of his calling, and what the
riches of the glory of his inheritance in the
saints, And what is the exceeding greatness
of his power to us-ward who believe, . . .*
(Ephesians 1:17-19).

When you match your vision with God's vision, He
will abundantly supply the resources and the power
regardless of your handicaps. I have one woman's
success story to tell you; you know I love success
stories! This lady, we'll call her Laura, found herself
divorced at the age of 45 with no specialized skills
or experience with which to earn a living for herself
or her teenage children. Now, I call that a "mid-life"
crisis. A "crash course" enabled Laura to get an office
job, but she was miserable. The business world was
not where she belonged.

After "throwing in the towel," but still needing to
eat, this displaced homemaker started cleaning
houses for an agency—and discovered she loved doing
it. However, this didn't happen until she stopped long
enough to humble herself and seek the face of God
for direction. Cleaning houses may not be your idea
of a vision from God, but let me tell you what

happened. God began replacing her low self-esteem with self-confidence; and after several months of working for others, Laura felt the Lord was telling her to start her own business.

The idea of her own business was overwhelming to Laura. She was without money or customers, but she knew that God's way was the best way. Testing the vision, Laura asked the Lord for the specific amount of money necessary for equipment to start her business. Soon after, a lady whom Laura had just met was impressed to give Laura a check. You guessed it; the check was within **two cents** of the amount for which Laura had prayed. I don't need to tell you that Laura soon had customers and is today the proud proprietor of a small but successful business. God is supplying Laura's needs, and she is happy and content.

CATCH A SPIRITUAL VISION

Thus far, I have not mentioned your *spiritual* vision. By that, I mean the place you desire in your relationship with the Lord and His Church. There could scarcely be anything more important in the whole of your life. Jesus said that we are to love God with our whole heart, soul, strength, and mind and our neighbor as ourself (see Luke 10:27). You will not have that kind of love without fellowshiping daily with the Lord. This involves reading and meditating on the Word as well as praying and listening to His voice. It also requires involvement in a local church body. Unless you are available to God and to other believers, the spiritual gifts God has for you will not operate through you.

Just as God has given to each of us certain *natural* talents and abilities, He has also given *spiritual* talents and abilities—or gifts. Romans 12:6-8 says that we have all been given a "motive" gift which "motivates" our Christian life and experience. It is every Christian's privilege to operate the spiritual gifts mentioned in I Corinthians 12:8-10 as the Holy Spirit chooses. Some of us have been given one of the ministry gifts spoken of in Ephesians 4:11. You see, the Lord has a vision of His Body ministering to one another, becoming strong and united, and telling the good news of Jesus Christ to the whole world:

> *But ye shall receive power, after that the Holy Ghost is come upon you: and ye shall be witnesses unto me both in Jerusalem, and in all Judea, and in Samaria, and unto the uttermost part of the earth* (Acts 1:8).

You may never have the kind of dreams or visions as did Joseph, a young Jewish slave who became a ruler in Egypt, or Daniel, the prophet who not only stopped the mouths of lions but also stopped the "prince of Persia" with his prayers. Nevertheless, you can have the kind of dreams and visions that put you over with God in this life. I trust you take the time to dream these kind of dreams and have these kind of visions. With *your* vision you can successfully plan

46

each day that God gives you with hope and joy. That is what I call maximizing your day God's way:

> . . . *your young men shall see visions, and your old men shall dream dreams: And on my servants and on my handmaidens I will pour out in those days of my Spirit; . . .* (Acts 2:17,18).

Chapter Three

HITTING THE MARK

THE VALUE OF SETTING GOALS

*Brethren, I count not myself to have apprehended: but this one thing I do, forgetting those things which are behind, and reaching forth unto those things which are before, I **press toward the mark for the prize** of the high calling of God in Christ Jesus* (Philippians 3:13,14).

In this chapter we will be discussing goals. No vision takes shape without goals. You must set goals in order to see your visions become realities; otherwise the visions will be just *castles in the air.* It takes goals to be able to "hit the mark." An archer chooses a target for his goal before shooting his arrows. Otherwise the archer will waste his time shooting arrows into "thin air." Without goals *you* will never hit the mark and your days will be filled with wasted time.

In II Kings 13:14-19 we read about Joash, one of Israel's kings who failed because he didn't know how to set goals. Joash was *overly* dependent upon the prophet Elisha. It appears that Joash always wanted Elisha to seek God for him, instead of having the confidence to seek God himself. Joash made Elisha his crutch instead of his godly counsel. God would have been pleased if Joash himself had set some goals.

Can you imagine Joash's distress when Elisha became deathly ill? What would Joash do without Elisha? At this time the land of Syria was a very real threat to Israel. Joash rushed to Elisha's bedside because Joash wanted the prophet to tell him what to do about the Syrians. The wise old prophet told Joash to open a window and take a bow and several arrows. "Shoot," Elisha said. When Joash shot the arrow, Elisha declared, "the arrow of the Lord's deliverance from Syria." Then Elisha told Joash to continue; Joash shot only three more arrows.

The prophet Elisha was furious with the king. The **Lord** had placed Israel's deliverance in the hands of Joash, but Joash had failed. Joash didn't have the courage to see that God would fulfill this goal, as He had promised, if only God had the cooperation of a king who would be bold and foresighted.

The zeal of Joash, as well as his goals, were represented in those arrows. Instead of accepting the Lord's promise of deliverance, the cowardly king was afraid of imposing on God. Elisha told Joash that if he had set his goals higher by shooting many arrows, Syria would have been conquered. Instead, Israel would have only three victories over the enemy; but that wasn't enough to win in the final outcome.

How high do *you* set your goals? Do you work at achieving your goals wholeheartedly? Don't be afraid to let the Lord lead you in setting good goals or aid you in achieving these goals! He is behind you 100 percent. The Bible has a promise from God to meet every need, and those promises are secured by the precious blood of Jesus. Get out there in life and win!

When you have a goal in mind, your hope is to see the goal fulfilled. That end result is the final goal which must be set. However, just as each day is measured off in minutes and hours, so your ultimate goal is measured off in smaller steps or stages. Each step is also a goal, equally important as the ultimate goal, but it is only a part in achieving the final result. The completion of these lesser goals will bring you to the moment when you accomplish the larger goal.

While you may just be starting on some goals, other goals may be nearing completion. The major goals in life are not completed in a day, or even a week. Some may take years and others may incorporate a lifetime. Such as the goal which Paul the apostle had in striving for the high calling of Christ Jesus. Nevertheless, each and every day is an opportunity to achieve some goals and work on others. How very important it is then to make the most of every day. That is maximizing your day—God's way.

Our lives are always in transition and change; nothing ever stays the same. Although we may face some unexpected changes in our lives, we can always be on top of the circumstances with God's guidance and help; and proper goal setting can make this possible. When we have a ''blueprint'' for our lives and we carefully and diligently follow that ''blueprint,'' each day will be a success leading to further success.

No sensible building contractor begins a house without a blueprint. If he does, it will be obvious to everyone in the end that there was no plan. You may smile at that; but, unfortunately, many individuals go through life without a plan and the end result is equally as disastrous as building without a blueprint. In fact it is a much greater tragedy, because the value of a house cannot be compared with the value of a life. The house, for whatever purpose, is temporary; the building of a life produces eternal results.

You may agree with what I'm saying, but perhaps you've made mistakes or you think your situation can't be changed. Are you, at midlife or even older, reaping the result of years without goals? Maybe you've just become a Christian and you see that your goals have all been wrong. Is it possible to get a fresh new start? Well, let me tell you about a man who did.

This man's name was Saul. At the height of his career, Saul had his eyes "opened" to see that he was building his life on the wrong goals. Saul had firmly set goals he thought were right, and he was ardently fulfilling them. However, his goals were all wrong, and that is as bad as having no goals at all. Have you guessed that I'm speaking of Saul, whose name Jesus changed to Paul? Believe it or not, that Paul is the great apostle Paul who wrote most of the New Testament! It certainly wasn't too late for him to set new goals and change his life.

As Saul, this "self-made" man was a very important Jewish leader who took counsel against the early

Christians and demanded that they be imprisoned or put to death for their "heresy." Saul was "living up" to his name which means to "require," "demand," and "take counsel." Saul, a big man in his own eyes, was very religious; but Saul had set goals which were totally out of God's will.

Nevertheless, Saul had a heart for God, and God used that "open door" to miraculously transform Saul into Paul, giving him *new* life and *new* goals. Paul, now small in his own eyes, quit doing things his way and sought only to do things God's way. Yes, *Paul* means "to quit, or to be small." It was this man who wrote, *"I press toward the mark for the prize of the high calling of God in Christ Jesus"* (Philippians 3:14). Jesus changed Paul's goals and gave him a brand new start in life.

Toward the end of Paul's life, he stated that he hadn't yet fully attained, but he was still "pressing on." You see, Paul was always expanding his vision and setting more goals. Most of us can scarcely imagine accomplishing what Paul accomplished for Christ; but when I come to the end of my earthly life, I intend to be able to say, as Paul said, *"I have fought a good fight, I have finished **my** course, . . . "* (II Timothy 4:7). God has set a course for every one of us and has given us the ability in the Holy Spirit to finish that course. There never will be another Paul; but then, there will never be another **you**:

> *Not as though I had already attained, either were already perfect: but I follow after, if*

that I may apprehend that for which also I am
apprehended of Christ Jesus (Philippians 3:12).
I have fought a good fight, I have finished
my course, I have kept the faith: Henceforth
there is laid up for me a crown of
righteousness, which the Lord, the righteous
judge, shall give me at that day: and not to
me only, but unto all them also that love his
appearing (II Timothy 4:7,8).

JESUS IS A GOAL SETTER

As a man, Jesus Christ was the greatest goal setter
who ever lived. He set goals throughout His earthly
life and ministry. The gospels are filled with accounts
of Jesus fulfilling one goal after another, as He healed
and delivered the people. Jesus had come to set the
captives free, but the final goal of Calvary was always
foremost in His thinking. Jesus rejected every
temptation which might have deterred Him from that
victory. When the Lord disclosed to His disciples the
events of His upcoming death, Peter rebuked Jesus
in horror; but Jesus turned to Peter and said. ''Get
thee behind me—*Satan*'' (see Matthew 16:23).

One of the most amazing things about Jesus' life
is that He fulfilled goals that had been set for Him,
centuries before, through the mouths of the prophets,
thus removing all doubt that He was Who He said He
was, the Lord's Messiah. His place and manner of
birth, the details and reason for His death, even

His ministry had all been prophesied in the Scriptures. When Jesus stood in the synagogue and read from Isaiah 61, He said, " . . . *This day is this scripture fulfilled in your ears"* (Luke 4:21). And Jesus made it very clear that His goals were always the Father's goals. He set His heart, mind, soul, and body to do the Father's will:

> *The Spirit of the Lord GOD is upon me; because the LORD hath anointed me to preach good tidings unto the meek; he hath sent me to bind up the brokenhearted, to proclaim liberty to the captives, and the opening of the prison to them that are bound; To proclaim the acceptable year of the LORD . . .* (Isaiah 61:1,2).
>
> *And it came to pass, when the time was come that he should be received up, he stedfastly set his face to go to Jerusalem,* (Luke 9:51).
>
> *. . . Father, if thou be willing, remove this cup from me: nevertheless not my will, but thine, be done* (Luke 22:42).

Jesus has goals for you too! Every promise in the Word of God is a goal you can reach. Jesus wants you saved, healed, and delivered. He wants you to walk in abundance. Jesus wants you to exercise authority over Satan and his kingdom. Jesus wants you to be free from anxiety and fear by living in His peace. Jesus wants you to be an overcomer!

I could go on and on, but I can sum it all up through these words of Paul:

Blessed be the God and Father of our Lord Jesus Christ, who hath blessed us with all spiritual blessings in heavenly places in Christ: Till we all come in the unity of the faith, and of the knowledge of the Son of God, unto a perfect man, unto the measure of the stature of the fullness of Christ (Ephesians 1:3; 4:13).

Have I convinced you that goals are really important? Your success depends upon the goals you set for yourself. If you don't plan to succeed, you have already planned to fail. If you are going to be an achiever, then you must not only set goals, you must also establish priorities. So, let's find out how to set goals and establish priorities.

SET SPIRITUAL GOALS

In order to be a *whole* person you need spiritual goals, personal and material goals, and intellectual goals.

A relationship with God is *the most important* thing in the life of any individual. Obviously, that relationship must be your first priority. A spiritual relationship with the Lord develops as goals are set and consistently kept:

. . . the true worshippers shall worship the Father in spirit and in truth: for the Father seeketh such to worship him (John 4:23).

I'm sure every person reading this has a best friend.

How did you and that person come to the point when you preferred one another above all your other acquaintances? You didn't just meet one day and *"zap,"* you were best friends. No, you developed a friendship by spending time together; and whether you were aware of it or not, you set goals regarding your relationship.

What holds true with a best friend, holds true with God. When you accepted Jesus as your Lord and Savior, you knew *about* Him but you didn't *know* Him. At that moment, you may or may not have been overwhelmed with an awareness of God's love, but you weren't really acquainted with Him. Most individuals accept Christ simply because they recognize their sin and see the truth of Calvary.

The late C.S. Lewis, a renowned intellect, author, *and* atheist was almost angry when he bowed his knee to Jesus. Mr. Lewis came to the fact of God's reality and saw that without a savior his sin would damn him to hell. However, through the years, Jesus became C.S. Lewis' best friend because Mr. Lewis spent time developing that relationship. He made that his goal.

If time is required to develop your relationship with the Lord, it is necessary to set goals as to how that time will best be spent. The length of time you spend with the Lord and the time of day you choose to spend it are also very important. You need to set goals for each aspect of your daily communion with God. There is no "formula," but there are some guidelines.

Personally, I prefer to spend the first part of the day with the Lord. There is **no** better way to get my day started than with Him. I must have fresh guidance daily, and I need God's wisdom in setting my goals for that day. If I were to start my day without that time with the Lord, I would be unequipped for the day's activities. I don't want to do my thing and then ask God to approve it; I desire to know God's will for my day and then set my goals accordingly. This way I will be an achiever:

> . . . *though our outward man perish, yet the inward man is renewed day by day* (II Corinthians 4:16).

The two major priorities for time with the Lord are His Word and prayer. Any good relationship is developed largely through conversation. God talks to us through His Word, and we talk to God through prayer. You will not only learn about God through His Word, but you will also learn about yourself. This is not a study on prayer, but it must be said that prayer is not a one-way conversation. It isn't just you talking to God; it is God speaking to you! Surprisingly enough, you can usually learn more by listening than by talking.

You may be wondering, "How will I find time for the Lord?" Let me tell you that you won't *find* time for the Lord; you will have to *make* time for the Lord. If you value your time as precious, then you will spend some of it with God. In today's hectic world everyone has a busy schedule; but I guarantee that when you make time for the Lord, He will make time for you. I'm sure there will be other moments during the day when you will talk to God and you will hear His voice, but there must be that special time in the day that is reserved only for Him and His Word.

If you haven't yet established a daily time with the Lord, you shouldn't "bite off more than you can chew." Don't defeat yourself by setting goals you can't attain. The determination to do *something* is the place to start, then begin to stretch the time. At first it may be only 10 to 15 minutes. Discipline yourself to that goal, and then begin to stretch your goal.

In the Garden of Gethsemane, Jesus told His disciples that if they spent one hour with Him in prayer, they would stand in the hour of temptation. That is a good formula, but don't think you've arrived if you pray one hour a day. Pastor Cho in Korea spends at least four hours every day in prayer and communion with the Lord.

Quality time with the Lord should be the foundation upon which all your goals are established and carried through. You will not have the wisdom to set accurate and successful goals without first hearing from the Lord. When you commit your way to the Lord, He will inspire you to reach for unattainable goals in the natural realm. In order to accomplish these goals, you will need the supernatural wisdom and energy that comes from time spent with God:

Now unto him that is able to do exceeding abundantly above all that we ask or think,

according to the power that worketh in us
(Ephesians 3:20).

Make the Lord and His Word your first priority, and He will set the rest of your priorities in order. God's desire is to fulfill you, not frustrate you. Listen to Him, and He will be your guide and director. God will give you a clear mind and clear direction. Not every detail will be spelled out from the beginning, but the Lord will lead you step by step to the completion of each of your goals:

Trust in the LORD with all thine heart; and lean not unto thine own understanding. In all thy ways acknowledge him, and he shall direct thy paths (Proverbs 3:5,6).

Most of you, I'm sure, are involved in a church fellowship; but others of you may not be. This, too, should be an important spiritual goal in your life. God has ordained that you should come under the authority and leadership of godly pastors and teachers, and it is imperative for God's children to have fellowship with their brothers and sisters in the Body of Christ. Don't try to live your Christian life as a loner; it won't work:

And let us consider one another to provoke unto love and to good works; Not forsaking the assembling of ourselves together, as the manner of some is; but exhorting one another: and so much the more, as ye see the day approaching (Hebrews 10:24,25).

The local church is God's instrument for blessing, protection, and the basic means by which the saints are equipped for service and ministry. The Lord may lead you to serve in other wonderful Christian groups and organizations, and that is good; but your local church should always be "home base." However, before you get too involved *outside* your church, find out where you may serve *within* the church. It may be singing in the choir, teaching Sunday school, working in the nursery, or sweeping floors.

SET PERSONAL AND MATERIAL GOALS

Having dealt with the spiritual goals of your life, let's go on to your personal and material goals. As was mentioned earlier in the chapter, you must know who you are. Self-awareness will help you set proper goals. If you are terrible at mathematics, obviously you will never make a good accountant. When you were created, God put into you certain personality traits and He gave you special abilities. These traits and talents were given to enable you to succeed in life. Following and developing these gifts will bring you to success, fulfillment, and happiness:

A gift is as precious stone in the eyes of him that hath it: whithersoever it turneth, it prospereth (Proverbs 17:8).

A man's gift maketh room for him, and bringeth him before great men (Proverbs 18:16).

61

You must be realistic about yourself when setting goals, but always keep in mind that the Lord wants to stretch you beyond your wildest imagination. I know a woman who received her formal education in the field of art. Betty's vision was to have an art career, and although she has enjoyed this talent and has sold some of her work through the years, it never became a vocation. God had other goals in mind. Interestingly, Betty had taken enough education courses in her senior year of college to graduate with a teaching certificate as well as the fine arts degree.

This lady taught briefly in public schools, but marriage and a family interrupted her career outside the home. However, Betty realized her talent for telling stories to her children; and soon a large group of youngsters would gather in her home every week to listen to Betty make Bible stories ''come alive'' for them. Betty found great delight in teaching the children and in seeing them eagerly give their little hearts to Jesus.

Through the years Betty developed her teaching skills, and after some time the Lord led her into teaching adult Bible studies. Then, ''by accident,'' Betty heard that her church intended to produce its own Sunday school curriculum. Betty was filled with the desire to be part of the project, so she volunteered to write and was accepted. This led to a very rewarding experience writing children's material, and later Betty was given the opportunity to write adult material. Today Betty is still enjoying the rewards and benefits of writing.

I want you to observe several important things about Betty's story and apply them in making and fulfilling goals in your own life. First, find ways to train and develop the skills and talents you know you have. Second, stay open to any opportunity the Lord may bring your way. Don't throw out any ideas and "urges" you may have before you've tested them and given them room to grow. Third, continually use your skills and abilities, and always be eager to learn more.

It isn't the "gifted" people or the people who "get the breaks" who are the achievers in life. Achievers are those who *set* the right goals and *keep* them. This requires hard work, diligence, determination, discipline and the ***proper use of time.*** It is impossible to use time wisely without setting goals for yourself. Ultimately, your level of accomplishment will be determined by the goals you have set.

SET PHYSICAL GOALS

At this point, let's talk about your physical goals. Our society has become extremely body-conscious. The racks in the stores are full of books and magazines telling us how to be healthy and have long life. Some of this material stresses exercise, some nutrition and diet, and still others recommend potions for the outside and the inside. We have walkers, joggers, runners, etc. Everyone wants to be physically fit. Someone said, "If I had known I was going to live so long, I would have taken better care of myself!"

There is no question that the Lord wants you to live a long, healthy life full of vigor and enthusiasm; and you can't do that without being physically fit. I recommend that you eat right and get enough exercise and rest. Take care of yourself! You'll never do your best if you are sick or in poor health. A physical fitness program must be planned to fit your own needs. Vocation, size, age, etc., will determine an exercise routine; but there are no limits on eating right. Good health is a part of running the Christian race:

> *For physical training is of some value, but godliness has value for all things, holding promise for both the present life and the life to come* (I Timothy 4:3 NIV).

PLAN YOUR DAYS AND SCHEDULE YOUR TIME

I have long-range goals for my life, but I also have short-term goals. I break all my goals into periods of time. Every year I set specific goals which I expect to achieve in that 12-month period. Then I set goals for each of those months. I also set weekly and even daily goals. Some of my daily goals are steps toward long-range goals, but there are always goals just for that day.

I like to name my days. When I give my day a name, even that name is a goal setter for achievement. Naming my day is not something I do lightly; I seek to know the mind of the Lord for my day. When I know that I'm facing a particularly difficult day, I may name that day, "my victory day." If I have a day with an unusually heavy schedule, that day may be "my achievement day." If I'm being tempted to worry about a matter, I can name that day, "peace." If my body is being attacked with sickness, that's my "healing day." I have joy days, wisdom days, love days, etc.

Not only do I name my day but I also choose scriptures that apply to the name and I speak them over my day. For example, if my day is "courage," some good scriptures would be Joshua 1:6, *"Be strong and of good courage: . . ."* and II Timothy 1:7, *"For God hath not given us the spirit of fear; but of power, and of love, and of a sound mind."* If it is my day to "possess my inheritance," I might choose II Peter 1:3: *"According as his divine power hath given unto us all things that pertain unto life and godliness, through the knowledge of him that hath called us to glory and virtue."*

Setting proper goals and fulfilling them takes planning. If you don't know what it is you want to do, there is no way you can set goals that will bring you achievement. Neither can you fulfill your goals if you are not properly prepared. I will illustrate this by telling a funny story on myself. It's about a bad habit I had: trying out new recipes on guests.

Once when we were expecting a dinner guest, I found a new recipe which sounded marvelous. I prepared the dish and proudly set it on the table. When our guest took the first bite, I noted with horror the strange expression on his face. To my embarrassment, the food was practically raw. I had made a mistake in the baking time. The guest was gracious; but from that time to this, I have never served company a dish that hasn't been tried and tested first. My goal was to serve our guest a delectable meal, but I was not properly prepared to do that.

Every choice you make is a goal you set. Bad choices set bad goals which produce bad results. I want you to make good choices, and be determined to settle for nothing less than excellence in whatever you do. The Holy Spirit will give you good ideas and guide you in making wise choices when you submit yourself to Him. Every good idea I get I write down. If I still like the idea after giving it prayerful consideration, I incorporate the idea into my goals.

You must always keep your goals in mind if you want to excel. I keep a record of all my goals. I never have to wonder what it is I need to do. I open my notebook and I have it laid out before me. I write down all the goals I have for each day, as well as recording my weekly, monthly, and annual goals. That way I never get side-tracked. When a goal is completed, I check it off my list and make room for other goals.

By now you may be thinking, "But I'm not perfect. Things don't always work out that way. I schedule my day, and then a dozen things interrupt my schedule.'' No, you are not perfect; and I know all about interruptions. I used to plan *every* minute of my day, and any interruption was a frustration. I prayed over my day, and there were still interruptions.

Even when my husband Wally asked me to lunch, I would be annoyed by the interruption. Then God began to teach me something; I could bind unnecessary interruptions, but I needed to schedule a certain amount of time everyday for important things which I could not foresee or plan. Now, when Wally asks me to lunch, I can go, relax, and have an enjoyable time being with him.

God has sent some unusual interruptions my way which have blessed and advanced my ministry. In 1977 the Lord told me to do a live TV broadcast from Cairo, Egypt. I questioned such a strange interruption in my schedule. My traveling ministry was in its infancy, and I couldn't understand the need to go overseas just to say a few words into a TV camera. Well, I obeyed the Lord, and I don't have space here to tell you of the miracles God performed on my behalf; but that act of obedience has opened doors for me that I could never have planned or even imagined.

Whether your goals are daily goals, yearly goals, or lifetime goals, make a point of sticking to them. That may be relatively simple for daily goals; but with goals that stretch out over a period of time, there is a temptation to let the work slide. Don't be like Scarlet O'Hara who had a habit of saying, "Oh, I'll think about that tomorrow."

When you apply yourself every day to the goals you have set, the discipline will reward you. Procrastination is one of the worst enemies of achievement. I'm sure you've heard the expression: "The road to hell is paved with good intentions." Good intentions never accomplish anything, but good works do. Put "legs" to your good intentions, and go places with them.

Approach every day as though it were the only day you have to achieve your goals and be a winner. In reality that is true. Yesterday is gone forever, and tomorrow isn't here. Nevertheless, yesterday is the foundation upon which you build today, and today is the foundation for tomorrow. Too soon, today will be gone and you will be faced with the day after. What you do today sets the stage for your future, for achievement or failure. Choose to be a winner:

> *Be ye doers of the word, and not hearers only, deceiving your own selves. But whoso looketh into the perfect law of liberty, and continueth therein, he being not a forgetful hearer, but a **doer of the work**, this man shall be blessed in his deed* (James 1:22,25).

We hear a great deal today about stress and how to handle it. Our society seems to be plagued with stress which manifests in confusion, frustration, anxiety, anger, fear, etc. Let me give you some valuable keys to stress management. Put God first, plan each day wisely, schedule your time—write it down, stick to your goals, and avoid delay. This will enable you to eliminate a great amount of stress.

God wants His saints to wear a happy face and walk in victory. He doesn't want them stressed out and under their circumstances. Remember, others are watching you. The world needs to see a different kind of person: an optimist instead of a pessimist, a winner not a loser, an *overcomer* rather than an *underachiever*. That person just might have the opportunity to lead others to Christ. Will you be that person? ''Goal setters'' can be ''soul getters'':

> *Now thanks to be unto God, which always causeth us to triumph in Christ, and maketh manifest the savour of his knowledge by us in every place* (II Corinthians 2:14).

Chapter Four

PROMISES, PROMISES, PROMISES

ALL GOD'S PROMISES ARE FOR YOU

Have you heard the old line, "Promises are made to be broken?" Has someone you care for made promises that have not been kept? Perhaps you feel your life has been "broken" because of someone's broken promises. If you have had any of these experiences, it may be difficult for you to believe that God will keep *His* promises. However, God has *never* broken a promise; and He never will!

Do you ever think that God might keep His promises to others but He would never do it for you? Then again, you may think that God is whimsical, keeping His promises sometimes but not other times for some mysterious reason. Perhaps you have read the Scripture and have isolated God's promises for only the time and circumstance when they were given.

Whatever your experience has been, or whatever you may think, I want to tell you that **God's Word is the most certain thing in existence.** God's Word is as sure as God Himself; and to every promise in His Word, God says *yes*. Then He punctuates the "yes" with the *exclamation point* of "Amen" or "so let it be." Jesus said it would be easier for heaven and earth to pass away than for God's Word to pass away (Luke 16:17). I want to emphasize that God has

71

forever expressed His mind and His will through His Word, and it is His Word of promise that gives us hope.

In II Corinthians 1:20 Paul, under the inspiration of the Holy Spirit, assured us that God will fulfill not some but **all** of His promises. They will be fulfilled because every promise is an expression of God's divine love for us, and every promise has been secured with the precious blood of Jesus Christ. Our Savior's blood is the guarantee. It truly can be said that God's promises are written in the blood of Jesus Christ. Do you think the Father would have given us His Son to secure the promises if He did not intend to keep those promises:

> *Think not that I* [Jesus] *am come to destroy the law, or the prophets: I am not come to destroy, but to fulfil. For verily I say unto you, Till heaven and earth pass, one jot or one tittle shall in no wise pass from the law, till all be fulfilled* (Matthew 5:17,18).

There are thousands of promises in the Word, and God declares emphatically that He will fulfill each and every one of them. May I say it this way? God promises to keep His promises. Every promise in God's Word is a gift from the Lord, beautifully wrapped in His abundant love. All God's children can share these gifts without ever diminishing them. Because the Lord is " . . . *the same yesterday, and to day, and for ever"* (Hebrews 13:8), I can assure you that He hasn't changed His mind about any of His gifts:

72

Every good gift and every perfect gift is from
above, and cometh down from the Father of
lights, with whom is no variableness,
neither shadow of turning (James 1:17).

Now I want you to notice that Paul said the promises made to us by God are fulfilled in our circumstances **by us**. Although God has the ability and the desire to bring every promise to pass in our lives, we each must individually appropriate the promises by faith. It is faith that moves God into action on our behalf. However, the God Who tells us it is our faith which activates His promises also inspires our faith through His Word. If we mix faith with the promise, we will receive the thing we ask for:

So then faith cometh by hearing and hearing
by the word of God (Romans 10:17).

In order to maximize your day God's way you must appropriate the promises which the Lord has given to you. Every day is a fresh new promise from the Lord, and every second in that day holds the promise of opportunity and fulfillment. Therefore it is vital that you know God's Word in order to know His will and His direction. Without a knowledge of God's promises, you will be unable to chart the course of your life or to make the most of the time God has given to you in each day. Each promise is a goal setter, and each promise holds the dynamic potential for achievement.

God's Word is the ''road map'' for your life; and when you take hold of the promises in the Word, the

Holy Spirit supplies the energy to travel that road without mishap or failure. Abraham, who is called the "father" of our faith, is one of the best illustrations of an individual following God's Word as a map. This great man of faith followed the map of God's Word all the way from the city of Ur in Chaldea to the Promised Land. Abraham's route took him some 700 miles from what is now southern Iraq into Israel, and the journey spanned several years.

Abraham had been busy following his own map when one day the Lord spoke to him and gave him a different direction. From that moment Abraham planned every day of his life in accordance with the promises which the Lord had given to him. Now you must understand that Abraham had not known the true and living God. This man lived in a land of idol worshipers; but when God spoke to Him, Abraham obeyed and changed the direction of his life.

Leaving a comfortable environment, Abraham stepped out into the unknown with only the promises of God. It wasn't always easy and it wasn't always comfortable, but it was certain. The reason the way was certain was because Abraham believed God. Abraham was no more perfect than you and I are; he made mistakes, but he always got back on course. That course was according to God's Word.

One of the most difficult things for Abraham to believe was God's promise of an heir. When God told Abraham he would have a son, Abraham and his wife Sarah were "up in years," even for a time when folks were living over a century. As a matter of fact, God waited until it was humanly impossible for either Abraham or Sarah to have this child. Nevertheless, for *25 years* the couple planned for a baby, and faith in God's Word produced the promised son—Isaac was born:

For when God made promise to Abraham, because he could swear by no greater, he sware by himself, Saying, Surely blessing I will bless thee, and multiplying I will multiply thee. And so, after he had patiently endured, he obtained the promise (Hebrews 6:13-15).

Do you have unfulfilled dreams? Are there plans you won't make because you can't see how they could ever come true? Then just look at Abraham and Sarah. If your desire is to please God, then I believe that it is God Who put the dream in your heart. If you will search the Scriptures for promises that answer your need, the Holy Spirit will show them to you. Then you can plan each day with your goal in mind and the promise in your heart. What God has done for anyone else, He will do for you:

Wherein God, willing more abundantly to shew unto the heirs of promise the immutability of his counsel, confirmed it by an oath: That by two immutable things, in which it was impossible for God to lie, we might have a strong consolation, who have fled for refuge to lay hold upon the hope set before us (Hebrews 6:17,18).

75

As I have mentioned before, God created you and He has a plan for your life that will bring blessing and satisfaction. God's way is always the best way, and God has expressed that way through His Word and His promises. Isn't it amazing that, although these promises have been given to every believer, no matter what the time or circumstance, God is able to cause certain promises to fit us individually according to our personality and our specific need at a particular time?

In whatever way you receive the Word into your mind, whether it is preached, spoken, or read, that Word is *logos*. However, when the Holy Spirit speaks that Word into your spirit, it then becomes *rhema*, filled with energy and power. In this way, the Lord fits a word or a promise to *you*. I'm sure you have had the experience of reading your Bible or hearing a sermon when a particular promise or portion of scripture "turned on" inside you as though someone had switched on an inner light. The Word became alive to you, and with that vitality came the energy of faith. That is *rhema*, a revelation of God's Word.

SIX STEPS TO DAILY APPLICATION OF THE WORD

All your visions, your goals, your plans, your schedules are subject to failure unless they are based on the solid foundation of God's Word. You will never get the most out of each day without that foundation. If you are going to maximize your day God's way, your plans and activities must be based on God's principles. Have you ever carefully laid out goals for the day, then spent the time "spinning your wheels," accomplishing very little? You may have realized later that you charged into the day without the counsel of the Lord or His Word.

It is one thing to know you need the Word; it is quite another thing to know how to apply the Word. In order to gain and maintain optimum benefit from your days, it is necessary to apply the Word so it works for you. Have you ever met an intellectual with a great deal of knowledge who had little or no ability to translate that knowledge into application? That person had no practical wisdom or "common sense."

I do not want you to lack the wisdom it takes to make use of God's Word. I'm going to give you six steps that will enable you to see God's promises fulfilled every day of your life. There is no question about the Word producing results when you discipline yourself diligently to apply it. I want to emphasize discipline and diligence. There is nothing magical about God's Word; it won't work just because you want it to work. Don't *try* the Word, *apply* the Word—constantly, consistently, and confidently!

1. HEAR THE WORD

The first step in this process is *hearing the Word*. This "hearing" requires time spent feasting on the Scriptures. The Lord has put a thirst and an appetite for His Word in the heart of every believer. The more you feed at His banquet table, the more your appetite will be whetted for God's *food*. Time spent daily by yourself in the Word is the very best way to gain knowledge of the Scriptures and the promises they contain. Of course, you can also hear the Word by attending church services, Bible studies, or by listening to Bible teachers on radio and TV:

> *As newborn babes, desire the sincere milk*
> *of the word, that ye may grow thereby: If so*
> *be ye have tasted that the Lord is gracious*
> (I Peter 2:2,3).

Some of your time with the Lord should also include meditation, memorization, and study. Give the Holy Spirit every opportunity to reveal the Truth. If you are going to plan your days in accordance with God's Word, it is necessary to gain an accurate understanding and revelation of what you read. Therefore, study and contemplation are invaluable. A wealth of wonderful books and commentaries are available to aid you in your study of the Scriptures:

> *Blessed is the man that walketh not in the*
> *counsel of the ungodly . . . But his delight*
> *is in the law of the LORD; and in his law*
> *doth he meditate day and night* (Psalm 1:1,2).

I have one caution concerning anything you ''hear'' apart from the Word of God itself. Be certain it agrees with the major truths of God's Word. If you are a new believer, it would be wise to have your pastor, Bible teacher, or a reputable Bible bookstore recommend good study material. Many Bibles have excellent study material. Beware of publications by a group or cult expounding their particular "revelation." Stay with writing which proclaims Jesus as the virgin-born Son of God, Who died for our sins, and bodily rose again in power and glory.

One of the most thrilling accounts of a life directed by hearing "the Word" is told in the book of Joshua. I'm talking about Rahab, a Canaanite woman who lived in the city of Jericho at the time when Israel first entered the Promised Land. Rahab didn't have a Bible to read, not even a small portion; but she did have ears to hear the news that spread all over Canaan about how God mightily delivered Israel out of the hand of the Egyptians.

Rahab is first introduced to us in the second chapter of Joshua. When Joshua, Israel's leader, sent two spies to "check out" the walled city of Jericho, they found lodging and protection in the house of Rahab, the harlot. Unfortunately, the spies were seen entering the city; but Rahab hid the men when the king's soldiers came to her home searching for the spies. Why should this woman of Canaan save the lives of men who were enemies of Jericho? Let Rahab herself answer that question:

> *And she said unto the men, I know that the LORD hath given you the land, and that your terror is fallen upon us, and that all the inhabitants of the land faint because of you. For we have **heard** how the LORD dried*

79

up the water of the Red Sea for you, when
ye came out of Egypt; and what ye did unto
the two kings of the Amorites, that were on
the other side of Jordan, Sihon and Og,
whom ye utterly destroyed (Joshua 2:9).

Rahab told the spies how the hearts of all her people melted with fear when they heard how the God of heaven and earth had delivered His people. There wasn't a man around who had any courage left to face Israel. Note that God had given Canaan into the hands of Israel from the moment they crossed the Red Sea, and yet the people of Israel were so busy looking at the giants in Canaan *they couldn't hear* God's Word, which promised them the land. Their unbelief cost them 40 years wandering in the wilderness. What a waste of time!

2. BELIEVE THE WORD

How people *hear* what they hear is so important. All the people of Canaan had been told of Israel's mighty deliverance by God's hand. In everyone's heart except Rahab's, the news instilled fear and dread; but when Rahab heard the same news her heart was filled with faith in Almighty God. Rahab took the second step; she believed. Like every other Canaanite, Rahab was involved in the worst kind of idolatry and sin, but what she heard caused her to turn her life around. Although the two Hebrews thought they were only spying out Jericho, the

Holy Spirit had sent them to locate a woman of faith who had decided to plan her days according to the Word of God.

The Israelites did take Jericho in the most miraculous way. Most of you probably know of the seven-day hike around the impenetrable walls of the fortress city. With only a shout of *faith* the walls came tumbling down; that is, all the walls except the portion upon which Rahab's home was built. She and her family were spared that day because Rahab heard truth, mixed it with faith, and obeyed the spies by marking her home with a scarlet rope. Rahab later married a Hebrew, and this woman who *had ears to hear* is listed in the genealogy of the Lord Jesus Christ.

3. TALK THE WORD

The third step in applying the Word is *talking the Word*. Once you have put God's Word in your heart and you've listened for the Holy Spirit's guidance, it is necessary to speak the Word over everything that concerns you—yourself, your days, your plans, and your schedule. God's children need to talk like their Father; it wasn't until God spoke His Word that creation came into being. Jesus resisted Satan's plans by speaking the Word. You too can direct your life and maximize your time by putting the Word in your mouth.

Whatever your plans, whatever your difficulties or obstacles, God's Word can make a way for you. This is why meditation and memorization of the promises in God's Word are so important. You need to know certain promises that answer your every need or circumstance. If you don't know the promises, you can't speak them; and if you don't speak the promises, nothing will happen in accordance with them. Put God's Word in your mouth and you will be an achiever:

And these words, which I command thee this day, shall be in thine heart: And thou shalt teach them diligently unto thy children, and shalt talk of them when thou sittest in thine house, and when thou walkest by the way, and when thou liest down, and when thou risest up (Deuteronomy 6:6,7).

Don't do as some people who contradict with their mouth every promise they say they believe. We've all heard someone say, ''Oh yes, I believe I'm healed by Jesus' stripes''; but then they proceed to talk about all their aches and pains. God's Word of promise has power to work in your life only when you agree with it. Say what you believe, and believe what you say:

. . . out of the abundance of the heart the mouth speaketh. A good man out of the good treasure of the heart bringeth forth good things: and an evil man out of the evil treasure bringeth forth evil things. But I say unto you, That every idle word that men shall speak, they shall give account thereof in the day of judgment. For by thy words thou shalt be justified, and by thy words thou shalt be condemned (Matthew 12:34-37).

If you abundantly store the good treasure of God's Word in your heart, you will speak out of that abundance and create your days the way you want them. God has given you the authority of His Word to rule your life and circumstances. If you are not speaking the Word, life and circumstances will rule you. Some folks think it's presumptuous to "claim" God's promises; but let me tell you if they don't speak the promises, they will speak against the promises. God calls that *"an evil heart of unbelief"* (Hebrews 3:12). You'll either be as positive as the Word or as negative as the world. You can't "straddle the fence" about God's Word and still expect to receive anything:

> *For let not that man think that he shall receive any thing of the Lord. A double minded man is unstable in all his ways* (James 1:7,8).

There are other people who are just leaving things in God's hands. These people are afraid if they start claiming promises and speaking them over their lives, they will heap God's blessing upon their lust. There is one sure way to know that won't happen; hide God's Word in your heart. The Lord tells us that when we delight in Him, He will give us the desires of our heart. Very simply, that means our desires will be in line with God's will when we delight in Him and His Word:

> *Delight thyself also in the LORD; and he shall give thee the desires of thine heart. Commit thy way unto the LORD; trust also in him; and He shall bring it to pass. And he shall*

*bring forth thy righteousness as the light, and
thy judgment as the noonday* (Psalms 37:4-6).

Years before I started the ministry God has given to me, I was challenged by one of the teenagers in our church. This young man showed me a notebook in which he had begun to write promises that spoke particularly to him. He was digging them out of the Word and listing them by topics in his notebook. There was a section on healing, a section on prosperity, a section on overcoming, and so on. That so stirred me, I began my own small notebook, and very soon there were several large notebooks.

As I put those promises in the notebooks, I was putting them in my heart and speaking them over everything in my life. Those notebooks were an invaluable aid in my teaching ministry. When I started traveling, those notebooks went with me and the Word of God poured out of my mouth. As the Word did its work, I saw lives changed, souls saved, bodies healed, and people prosper and grow in the Lord.

Let me tell you about two remarkable people found in the New Testament who had faith to "create" things with their mouths. Matthew 8:5-10 tells of a Roman centurion who came to Jesus on behalf of his gravely ill servant. Jesus was willing to go to the centurion's home; but the centurion said, " . . . *speak the Word only, and my servant shall be healed*" (Matthew 8:8). This military leader understood the power of words spoken by someone with authority. The servant was healed and Jesus remarked that He hadn't seen such faith in all of Israel.

The other person who created a miracle with her mouth was the woman with an issue of blood. You can read about her in Mark 5:25-34. This woman had hemorrhaged for 12 years, and no physician could help her, but she heard about Jesus. In spite of a large crowd, this sick woman pushed through to the Healer saying " . . . *If I may touch but his clothes, I shall be whole"* (Mark 5:28). The instant the woman touched Jesus she *was* healed, and the Lord commended her faith, enough to speak her miracle into being.

4. WORK THE WORD

The action of the woman whose hemorrhaging was stopped leads to the fourth step in using the Word of God. That step is *working the Word.* It isn't enough to hear the Word, believe the Word, or even speak the Word; you must work the Word. Notice the progression of faith in this lady who received such a miraculous healing. First she heard about the healing power of Jesus and she believed; next she spoke what she believed, and then she put her faith into action. When she worked the Word, it worked for her. This woman would never have received what she needed if she hadn't acted out what she believed—and neither will you. Faith requires action.

I am reminded of another lady who also did a remarkable thing. This lady accepted an invitation to go to Africa with a Christian friend. The purpose of the trip was to visit several mission stations. During the tour both the women were asked to bring some message to the people. One woman wondered what she might say that would encourage these African Christians. To her amazement when this woman prayed about it, the Holy Spirit told her to exhort the people on the subject of tithing.

These African people were very poor, and the woman thought that to speak on tithing would be inappropriate. How could these poor people tithe on their meager substance? Surely God wouldn't ask these people to tithe, she reasoned. Nevertheless, the Holy Spirit continued to impress this subject on her heart. When the time came to speak, the woman obeyed the Spirit and started a wave of prosperity among those ''poor'' people. You see, the only people who are truly poor are those who do not act upon the Word of God.

The Lord promises to rebuke the devourer for our sakes when we tithe and to pour out such a blessing upon us that we can't contain it all (Malachi 3:10,11). If the missionary woman, acting on compassion rather than the Word, had been unwilling to teach His people about tithing, they would have been robbed of their blessing. But when these Africans heard the Word, they willingly acted upon it. They brought chickens, eggs, handmade items—anything they had they tithed. Soon the Lord began to prosper these people because they believed and obeyed the promise. Praise God, the Word works all over the world for those who work it.

5. WALK THE WORD

The fifth step necessary for seeing the promises of God fulfilled in your life is *walking the Word*. You must have consistency in your walk with the Lord as you apply God's promises to your life. This is the only way to maximize all your days God's way. Consistency paves the way to success. You can't expect to succeed if you apply the principles of God's Word one day but not the next. *Each day* claim promises that create a framework for accomplishment, and then live a righteous life in accordance with the Word.

Sometimes when things are going great, Christians get lazy about the Word and sloppy in their living. Others give up on the Word when things go particularly badly. These people are heading for some nasty bumps along the way. Please *don't* think I'm saying that if you live by the Word you'll never encounter difficulty. I *am* saying that you will *overcome* the difficulty when you confidently and consistently make the Word your rule.

Never say the Word isn't working! Always judge your circumstances by God's infallible Word; do not judge the Word by your circumstances. There are those who turn loose of God's promises when they don't see situations change in their lives. If your difficult situation looms bigger in your eyes than the Word, you will fail; but if you keep speaking the Word with faith and patience and *act* as though you believe it, that mountain will eventually move:

87

For verily I say unto you, That whosoever shall say unto this mountain, Be thou removed, and be thou cast into the sea; and shall not doubt in his heart, but shall believe that those things which he saith shall come to pass; he shall have whatsoever he saith (Mark 11:23).

The most graphic example in Scripture of someone walking on the Word is in the life of the apostle Peter. Who hasn't heard of Peter walking on the water? But *was it the water* upon which Peter walked? Let me refresh your memory concerning this incident found in Matthew 14:22-31. At evening the Lord Jesus had given His disciples orders to cross the sea of Galilee ahead of Him by boat. Jesus then went to a mountain to pray. Night came before the disciples reached the other shore, and with the night came a terrible storm.

In the midst of the storm, Jesus came walking across the sea toward the frightened men. At the sight of Jesus, the men were even more frightened because they thought they were seeing a ghost. Jesus called to the men and said, " . . . *Be of good cheer; it is I; be not afraid."* Whether it was wisdom or not, Peter responded with, " . . . *Lord, if it be thou, bid me come unto thee on the water."* At Jesus' Word, **"Come"**, Peter stepped out of the boat and *started* walking to Jesus.

Peter was actually walking *by faith on the Words of Jesus.* However, when Peter took his eyes off Jesus and began to look at the winds and the waves, the water no longer sustained Peter. Fear of the storm, rather than Jesus' Words, now controlled Peter; and he began to sink below the waves. Of course the Lord saved Peter when he cried for help, and together Jesus and Peter walked to the boat. Nevertheless, Jesus rebuked Peter saying, "... *O thou of little faith, wherefore didst thou doubt?*"

If Peter had been *consistent* in "his walk" that night, then the violent sound of the wind and the sight of the mountainous waves would not have hindered him. But let's not criticize Peter. Who among us has walked on water? At least Peter stepped out of the boat; and with a helping hand from the Lord, Peter was able to continue his walk. We all face tempestuous storms at one time or another in our lives, but an abiding faith in God's Word will carry us through just as certainly as *The Word* carried Peter that stormy night. If you think you're sinking, call on Jesus:

> *Abide in me, and I in you. As the branch cannot bear fruit of itself, except it abide in the vine; no more can ye, except ye abide in me. I am the vine, ye are the branches: He that abideth in me, and I in him, the same bringeth forth much fruit: for without me ye can do nothing ... If ye abide in me, and my words abide in you, ye shall ask what ye will, and it shall be done unto you* (John 15:4,5,7).

What a tremendous promise! Abiding in Jesus amounts to consistency in your life, and consistency produces achievement and success. Life without results is futile, but life lived in the promises of God is fruitful. Both consistency and productivity in your Christian walk are testimonies to the world that Jesus Christ is real and God is good. If we talk the Word, we must also walk the Word; otherwise we are hypocrites who seldom or never experience the reality of God's promises. In Matthew 23 hypocrisy produced only failure and ridicule:

> *But the wisdom that is from above is first pure, then peaceable, gentle, and easy to be intreated, full of mercy and good fruits, without partiality, and without hypocrisy* (James 3:17).

6. EXPECT MIRACLES

There is one final point I want to emphasize regarding the promises in God's Word. Expect the promises to produce miracles, and keep your focus on the supernatural. God's Word is alive with God's dynamic power, and every promise will produce supernatural results that can never be produced in the natural. God expects you to do what you can do, and then He will do what you can't do. Don't limit yourself to human ability, knowledge, wisdom, or experience; but lift yourself by faith into the limitless heights of God's divine ability, hang on tightly to the promises, and *look for miracles.*

Little David was just a boy when he faced the mighty giant Goliath to defend the nation of Israel; but when

David looked up toward the giant, his gaze went far beyond that towering head. David focused on heaven where he knew God was ready to fulfill every covenant promise given to His people. All the trained armies of Israel were there that day with King Saul, who stood a head taller than any of his men; but not one of them was willing to encounter Goliath in combat. Those cowards focused on Goliath's size instead of God's Word and permitted a boy to challenge the giant.

The fight was so mismatched that there was no way David could come out the winner—except for one thing. David challenged Goliath with the Word of God. The young man expected a miracle when he said:

> . . . *Thou comest to me with a sword, and with a spear, and with a shield: but I come to thee in the name of the LORD of hosts, the God of the armies of Israel, whom thou hast defied. This day will the LORD deliver thee into mine hand; and I will smite thee, and take thine head from thee; . . . that all the earth may know that there is a God in Israel* (I Samuel 17:45,46).

Goliath hurled curses at David that day; but David threw just one well-aimed stone from his sling—and it hit the mark. Goliath fell because of the crushing blow to his forehead, and David cut off the giant's head with Goliath's own sword. Israel won the battle that day because of one young boy who trusted God for miracles. With God's promises, you, too, can come out the winner in all of life's experiences. Hear the Word, believe the Word, talk the Word, work the Word, walk the Word—and expect miracles. Every day will be a victory.

Chapter Five

THE PRESSURE COOKER

LIFE BRINGS PRESSURE

*All things are lawful unto me, but all things are **not expedient**: all things are lawful for me, but I will not be brought under the power of any* (I Corinthians 6:12).

And herein I give my advice: for this is expedient for you, who have begun before, . . . perform the doing of it; that as there was a readiness to will, so there may be a performance also out of that which ye have (II Corinthians 8:10,11).

If ever there was a man *on course* and *on time* it was Paul, the apostle; and Paul continually exhorted other Christians to keep focused on their goals and not to allow the pressures of life to interfere. As for himself, Paul knew that winning the lost to the Lord Jesus Christ and strengthening the Church was his primary goal, and he refused to allow anything to stop him. Paul certainly was a person who demonstrated the ability to maximize every day God's way! Perhaps spending his early years "off course" made Paul more aware of the value of time.

Don't think that Paul did exceptional things just because he had a very special anointing and call. Yes, Paul did have a unique call and an anointing to fulfill that call, but so does each one of us. God is no respecter of persons; whatever *your* call in life, God has a special grace to enable *you* to be an achiever. Paul was never boasting when he challenged believers to follow his example, because Paul knew it was by the power of the Holy Spirit that he followed Jesus' example. In his writing Paul laid out guidelines for success and he laid out guidelines for failure. We all have a choice to make:

> *But unto every one of us is given grace according to the measure of the gift of Christ* (Ephesians 4:7).

In this chapter we are going to examine the pressures that keep us from maximizing our time and frustrate the fulfulling of our goals. Even when goals are set and schedules are made it often seems everything that could happen happens to prevent us from using our time efficiently and effectively. It takes wisdom and determination to keep on schedule.

There are three major enemies of time with which one must deal on a daily basis: the devil, the circumstance, and the flesh. Satan will do all that he can to mess up your circumstances and appeal to your flesh because his aim is to tarnish your testimony for Jesus and bring you to failure.

Let's take a look at Paul again. Did Paul succeed because he was exempt from life's problems? Was Paul so unique that none of these things ever touched him? Those questions must certainly be answered with an emphatic **no**. Few persons have ever encountered the problems Paul encountered as Satan attempted to keep Paul from fulfilling the task to which he had dedicated himself. Listen to Paul:

> *. . . in labours more abundant, in stripes above measure, in prisons more frequent, in deaths oft. Of the Jews five times received I forty stripes save one. Thrice was I beaten with rods, once was I stoned, thrice I suffered shipwreck, a night and a day I have been in the deep; In journeyings often, in perils of waters, in perils of robbers, in perils by mine own countrymen, in perils by the heathen, in perils in the city, in perils in the wilderness, in perils in the sea, in perils among false brethren; In weariness and painfulness, in watchings often, in hunger and thirst, in fastings often, in cold and nakedness. Besides those things that are without, that which cometh upon me daily, the care of all the churches*

(II Corinthians 11:23-28).

Have you ever wondered why the Lord just doesn't take away all the problems that steal your time and make you feel as though you are in a pressure cooker? The apostle Paul did. Three times Paul begged the Lord to take away the "thorn in his flesh." I believe the "thorn" that troubled Paul the most was the interference of religious people, both Jews and pagan, who continually stirred up trouble for Paul wherever he went to preach the gospel. Notice how many times Paul mentions trials at the hands of men (II Corinthians 11:23-28).

Although God revealed to Paul why he ran into so much difficulty, He did not remove the difficulties. The Lord did something better; He reminded Paul of the grace which would enable him to overcome in every problem situation. Satan put all the thorns in Paul's path because Paul was preaching the revelation of Christ and the Church wherever he went and multitudes were being born again into the kingdom of God. The devil tried to do everything he could to stop Paul, but he didn't succeed.

Even when Paul was repeatedly beaten and even shipwrecked, this man of God determined not to make a shipwreck of his life. He overcame by grace. Grace is a word often used among Christians; we talk about it, sing about it, and praise God for it. But what is this grace which God extended to Paul and to every other believer? A very simple acrostic explains that GRACE is God's Riches At Christ's Expense. Through grace the Lord extends to us His availability in protection, provision, and power. Grace exemplifies God's love as He offers His children the sufficiency of everything He is in order to meet our every need and to bring success in every situation:

> *And he* [God] *said unto me, My grace is sufficient for thee: for my strength is made perfect in weakness. Most gladly therefore will I rather glory in my infirmities, that the power of Christ may rest upon me* (II Corinthians 12:9).

96

Not even the Lord Jesus Christ was exempt from the pressures of daily interferences, temptations, and problems. That may surprise you, but Hebrews states that Jesus was tempted in *every* way just as we are. Luke 4:13 tells us that Satan sorely tempted Jesus at the very beginning of his ministry and even then the evil one left our Lord alone for only brief periods of time. Jesus was never immune to the devil's interference. This is the reason Jesus can understand and care about those things that trouble us, and He is the One Who will always have an answer to our dilemmas.

> *For in that he himself hath suffered being tempted, he is able to succour them that are tempted. . . . For we have not an high priest which cannot be touched with the feeling of our infirmities; but was in all points tempted like as we are, yet without sin* (Hebrews 2:18, 4:15).

MAKE GOD YOUR FIRST PRIORITY

Have you, like Paul, realized that you can't handle pressure or problems by yourself? There is no one in this world so wise, so powerful, so experienced, so organized, so wealthy, or so favored who can manage every day of his or her life without help. Recognizing our *inability* is the gateway to receiving God's *ability*. Don't try to manage your life in your own strength; it won't work. Paul said that when he offered God his weakness, God poured in His strength; when he acknowledged his infirmities, God "clothed" him with power. Paul was content to glory in Christ rather than in himself. What a powerful key to success and fulfillment:

Therefore I take pleasure in infirmities, in reproaches, in necessities, in persecutions, in distresses for Christ's sake: for when I am weak, then am I strong (II Corinthians 12:10).

You can see that Paul was a person whose life was totally dedicated to Jesus. From the moment of his conversion, Paul decided that every minute of every day belonged to God. For Paul, Christ was Lord of everything: his plans, his experiences, his very existence. Although Paul was presented with many trials, he avoided defeat when the pressure increased by knowing his days and his time really belonged to God. There was never any struggle or confusion in Paul's mind or heart about Who was boss. Paul eliminated a lot of pressure from his life because he made God his first priority.

Is your time yours, or is it the Lord's? You can avoid a great deal of internal pressure by deciding to live for God and not for self. A decision to make God your first priority will also keep you in victory when external pressures come against you. An experience of my own will illustrate this point. I was flying to a large convention; and because of a tight time schedule, I had worn the lovely silk dress I intended to wear when I spoke at the meeting that evening.

Directly ahead of me in the plane was a mother with a small baby. When our dinner trays were served, the woman couldn't eat because her baby was extremely fussy. I wasn't thrilled when the Lord told me to hold the baby so the mother could eat her meal in peace. I said, "Oh Lord, what if that baby spits up on my dress?" The Lord reminded me that the time I spent ministering to that woman could be as important as the time spent ministering to a whole convention. Humbled, I offered my help to the sincere gratitude of the baby's mother; and, of course, the Lord kept the baby's stomach quiet and my silk dress clean!

Priorities are so important, aren't they? When you commit your precious time and your precious things to God, He will multiply your time and protect those things you hold dear; and He will do it in such exciting and supernatural ways. However, if you try to hold on to these things, you will really put yourself in the pressure cooker. Don't give "the thief" an opportunity to fill your days with confusion and frustration. Don't let him steal the things you value. God's ways are so much better than our ways:

> *The thief cometh not, but for to steal, and to kill, and to destroy: I am come that they might have life, and that they might have it more abundantly* (John 10:10).

Why should any of us struggle to exchange our ways for His ways? When we wait on the Lord, He lets us in on secrets of wisdom and advice which we would never obtain any other way. If you are having difficulty sorting out the priorities in your life and in your days, make God your first priority and *He will set all your other priorities in order.* The Lord is so eager and willing to show us all how to maximize our days His way. He longs to demonstrate His power and ability in our lives and to deliver us from the pressures of life.

When I think of individuals who have overcome in times of great pressure, I am reminded of three men who found themselves in a *very real* pressure cooker. Most of us have heard this Bible story from Daniel 3, but let me refresh your memory about these young Jews who had totally committed their days to God and His commands. The people of Judah had been carried into captivity by the Babylonians whose king, Nebuchadnezzar, tried to force them to worship him and the Babylonian idols. Nevertheless, there were three notable Jews in the kingdom who refused the king's order; and that's how these young men found themselves in the pressure cooker.

You see, Nebuchadnezzar had erected an immense golden image; and he commanded everyone to fall down and worship this image. However, there was only one God in the hearts of Shadrach, Meshach, and Abed-nego; and they refused to bow before the idol even though the king made a decree that anyone who didn't bow would be thrown into a huge, fiery furnace. The king heard of the men's ''disobedience'' and gave them a second chance to worship the idol, but they still refused the king's command:

> . . . *our God whom we serve is able to deliver*
> *us from the burning fiery furnace, and he*
> *will deliver us out of thine hand, O king.*
> *But if not, be it known unto thee, O king,*
> *that we will not serve thy gods, nor worship*
> *the golden image which thou hast set up*
> (Daniel 3:17,18).

In a fit of rage, Nebuchadnezzar had the three men bound with ropes and thrown into the furnace heated seven times hotter than usual. Then the king sat back to watch. Nebuchadnezzar's eyes nearly popped out of his head when he looked into the furnace, and there were the three young Hebrews loosed and walking about with one Who looked like the **Son of God**. The king had seen the soldiers who threw the Jews into the furnace burned to death because of the intense heat. Yet, there were the three, whom the king intended to kill in his "pressure cooker," very much alive.

Does it pay to commit your days to God and allow Him to set your priorities in order? Well, when those three faithful young men walked out of that furnace, they didn't even smell of smoke although the fire had burned off the ropes that bound them. The experience also transformed a haughty, godless king. Listen to his words:

> . . . *Blessed be the God of Shadrach, Meshach,*
> *and Abed-nego, who hath sent his angel, and*
> *delivered his servants that trusted in him,*

and have changed the king's word, and yielded their bodies, that they might not serve nor worship any god, except their own God (Daniel 3:28).

PROBLEMS WHICH CREATE PRESSURE

Often when people are under great stress, I find that they are their own worst enemies. Let's find where we undermine ourselves and learn how to relieve the pressure. No one wants to set himself up for failure. On the contrary, each one of us, as a Christian, desires to know what it takes to use each day in such a way that we will be a blessing to God and others. We also desire to achieve personal success and a sense of well being.

One handicap to achievement can often be attempting to overachieve. Every person must set realistic goals for himself in order to succeed. If we overburden ourselves either on a daily basis or on a long-term basis, we are "setting ourselves up" for a "let down." Although quantity is important, quality is much more important. When we learn to pace ourselves and stick to a realistic schedule, with realistic goals, we will enjoy the fruits of meeting the schedules and accomplishing the goals.

While more aggressive people may tackle tasks which are beyond their abilities or take on too many responsibilities, less aggressive people may never be willing to challenge their time or abilities. These individuals are often content to let others succeed or excel, when they are quite capable of doing more than they are willing to try. The loss of satisfactory achievement will eventually put pressure on these individuals' self-esteem. Don't overdo, but don't under do. Either way, you will put pressure on yourself.

Trying to be someone you are not will certainly put you under pressure. Imitating the accomplishments of others or competing with those whose achievements you admire is never wise. God made only one you, and He has given you special attributes and abilities that are uniquely your own. The Lord doesn't want you to be a cheap imitation of someone else; He wants you to be an original. I have previously said a great deal concerning your need to discover yourself, so I won't deal with that issue at any length here. However, I will say that if you haven't spent time analyzing who you are, with the help of the Holy Spirit, there is no better time than now to do it.

Attempting to do things for which one is unqualified reflects another aspect of setting unrealistic goals. Because we all have certain limitations, we need to take them into consideration. Some of these limitations may be in training, talent, skill, age, location, etc. You need to know your limitations as well as your abilities when setting goals or even planning a daily schedule. For instance, some people have the ability to work very rapidly and still do a good job; others may be slow and methodical.

One person may plan too little and be bored; the other may plan too much and be frustrated. Plan your days for achievement.

No amount of effort or organization will bring success when you attempt to work in areas for which you are not suited. Of course, many limitations can be altered. If a certain amount of education or specialized training is within your reach and qualifies you to do something you desire to do, then by all means, go for it. However, if you long to be an opera star and you croak like a frog, forget it. That is not meant to be rude or critical, but it does illustrate my point.

Too often an individual who is willing to work is given a job for which he or she is unsuited. This person might do an excellent job in another area, but may fail to do well in the area in which he or she is placed. This can only lead to pressure and disappointment for all concerned. I have seen this happen in churches when volunteer workers are placed wherever there is a need. Pastor, Sunday school superintendent, don't make this mistake. If you are a supervisor, manager, or leader, be careful to place those under you in positions where they can be productive and happy. Keep the machinery running by putting the parts where they belong, and avoid unnecessary pressure.

Never before has a society been made more aware of the pressure one may experience as a result of past emotional or physical hurts and abuse. For whatever reason, many people have a mind-set that they can never succeed in anything. If you are one of those people, I want to tell you that God doesn't make junk! There isn't a person alive who does not have some God-given quality that will enable him or her to enjoy achievement in some area. Although there are individuals who need professional help, the best counsel anyone can receive is to take every past hurt to the Cross of Jesus Christ, find forgiveness for yourself and others, and put the past under the blood of our precious Savior. Then let Jesus and His Word heal you:

> *For God did not give us a spirit of timidity—of cowardice, of craven and cringing and fawning fear—but [He has given us a spirit] of power and of love and of calm and well-balanced mind and discipline and self-control* (II Timothy 1:7 The Amplified Bible).

For some of you, the limitations which put you in the pressure cooker are purely physical. You may have been born with a physical handicap, or the handicap may have been acquired through some sort of accident. Whatever the case, the problem exists and must be considered in determining realistic goals and in making schedules that can be achieved. Again, our present society is more aware than ever of this kind of limitation and has made great strides in opening many jobs and skills to the physically handicapped. Don't allow even this sort of limitation to keep you from being an achiever, and don't forget that Jesus is the great physician with supernatural healing power.

HAVE A PLAN FOR EVERY DAY

Have you taken a careful look at the everyday things that demand your time? Without a satisfactory awareness of those things which are a part of your routine, you can never organize your life or keep on a schedule that is both challenging and fulfilling. You need to make a list of all the activities you incorporate in your life. Some of these you will do everyday, some only weekly, some monthly, and some even less often; but everything which occupies your time needs to be included.

After making this list, I want you to analyze each activity on the list. Do you see things on that list which you can eliminate? I find that most people can save more time than they ever imagined by simply omitting activities that are neither necessary nor productive. I don't mean that you should allow no time for pleasure or relaxation. The old adage is still true: "All work and no play makes Jack a dull boy." However, much time is often wasted doing unnecessary things. I want you to eliminate the unnecessary demands on your time.

Don't allow illegitimate demands to rob you of valuable time and to throw you off schedule. Save your time for those activities you view as legitimate. It is not only necessary to make this determination concerning everything you routinely do but also it is vitally important to have the wisdom to decide what is legitimate and what is not when unplanned things arise. Meditating on God's Word and committing each day to the Lord is the best way I know to " . . . *be instant in season, out of season . . .* " (II Timothy 4:2). When interruptions of any sort arise, the Holy Spirit will give you the wisdom to decide whether the demand has a legitimate right to your time.

Obligation is an illegitimate time robber that puts subtle demands on many people. Be careful that you do not allow others to obligate you to tasks that neither God nor you deem necessary. Some individuals find it very difficult to say "No" when an activity seems valid or the person who asks has a need. Always be sure to get the mind of the Lord on any matter and not someone else's "good" ideas. If you do choose to accept a responsibility, make certain it is what you should do. Don't be afraid to refuse a job. If the task is not for you, it will waste your time, put you under pressure, and probably contribute to some other person's irresponsibility.

In order to have a workable plan for each day, you need to estimate the time it takes to accomplish each of your activities. After determining what activities are necessary and the amount of time it will take to accomplish them, put your plan on paper. The best way to conserve time and keep on course is to have a written schedule. Planning your day on paper is a very important way to avoid stress and pressure.

There are many good materials on the market to aid you in making out a schedule, so choose something that suits your particular needs.

I find a written schedule to be a very beneficial point of reference; in fact, I could not work successfully without it. For one thing a written schedule reduces the possibility of forgetting the tasks which I have planned. I also have found that I am much less apt to let things slide when I put them in writing. There is a greater degree of commitment to my tasks and my day when I have a visible plan in front of me. That plan keeps me on schedule and assists me in getting optimal benefit from my time. Time wasted is something I cannot tolerate.

At this moment you may be thinking that you are glad you do not work for me, but I'm not really a bear. On the whole, I find our staff to be happy and satisfied; and a big reason for this is because we maximize our days through proper scheduling. I take very seriously the opportunity to impact lives for Jesus Christ, and I place great value on every penny which my partners give into our ministry. Together we are serving the Lord, and this opportunity is measured in time. Therefore, efficient scheduling is a must. Without it there would be confusion, discontent, wasted money, wasted time, and wasted lives. Lack of organization is deadly!

Two of the greatest enemies of time, schedules, and achievement are *lack of discipline* and *procrastination*. These ''twins'' are probably responsible for more pressure in people's lives than anything I know. It is so easy to put things off until a "more convenient" time. When distractions, interruptions, and pressures come, you must be disciplined enough to stick to your schedule. If you find something unexpected is important enough to demand your time and attention, reschedule as soon as possible any task that you may not have time to complete that day.

I can think of no one who ever put himself under more pressure than Samson because he refused to discipline either his life or his time. Samson's tragic story is told in Judges 13-16. From the moment of his birth, Samson had everything going for him; but he wasted most of his days by serving self and never getting around to God's program. Samson was a son of promise—chosen by God for a special purpose before he was born. Nevertheless, Samson had to agree with God and choose that good purpose before it would come to fruition in his life. This is true for every one of us. Success and fulfillment do not come automatically; we have to cooperate with God every day.

Samson's story began at a time when Israel, because of sin, was under great pressure from the Philistines. The entire nation of Israel had failed to make God its first priority, and most of the people were doing whatever seemed right in their own eyes. Then God intervened, and the angel of the Lord paid a visit to a godly Hebrew woman. A son, who was to be a judge and deliverer in Israel, was promised to this childless woman and her husband Manoah. At Manoah's request the angel returned to give them instructions on how to train the promised son. This couple desired to make every day count in raising their child in God's way.

From his youth Samson knew what direction his life should take, but he was not wholly committed to God's plan. Samson didn't care a thing about maximizing his days God's way. Even though the Holy Spirit clothed Samson with supernatural strength, he chose to waste this strength on foolish pranks. A lust for the wrong women eventually spelled Samson's downfall. When the treacherous Philistine harlot, Delilah, won the heart of the foolish young man, she tricked him into disclosing the source of his strength:

> . . . *There hath not come a razor upon mine head; for I have been a Nazarite unto God from my mother's womb: if I be shaven, then my strength will go from me, and I shall become weak, and be like any other man* (Judges 16:17).

Samson had been dedicated to God at his birth and he wore his hair long as the mark of a Nazarite vow. Samson's long hair was the *outward* symbol of *inner* strength, but Samson had unwittingly and carelessly forfeited that supernatural gift of God. While Samson slept in her arms, Delilah robbed him of his strength by cutting his hair. Then she called in a band of Philistines to take him captive.

Although Samson had previously escaped from the strongest Philistines, he found himself powerless against them now. These wicked people put out Samson's eyes and forced him to work like an animal grinding grain in the prison. Because of an undisciplined life, Samson had totally lost sight of righteous goals; and he ended up losing not only his strength but also his physical sight. In the darkness, Samson, whose name means *sunlight*, began to "see the light"; and as his hair began to grow so did his strength. One day at a heathen celebration, the Philistines brought Samson out of prison to make sport of him. Little did they know that Samson, whose priorities finally lined up with God's, was a renewed man inside and out.

At Samson's request the young boy who was leading Samson placed him between the two huge pillars of the building that housed all the people. Knowing that it would be the last thing he would ever do, Samson gripped the pillars and with one enormous tug, pulled down the building. In Samson's death, he killed more Philistines than in his squandered lifetime. Samson had straightened out his priorities, but not until it cost him his life. How very sad it is that this person who was ordained to do mighty things for God wasted his days and his opportunities because he continually "put off" doing the right thing due to an undisciplined lifestyle.

You may be one of those people who is still procrastinating about making a schedule. Maybe you dislike the idea of being a slave to a plan. I can't begin to tell you how much pressure can be eliminated in your day by taking the time to schedule your time. When you do, you will find that time is your friend and not your enemy. Perhaps you have a schedule, but you neglect to put certain jobs or activities on the schedule because they are things you'd rather not do. Avoiding these things will not make them go away. Discipline yourself to fit that task into your schedule and get it done. Letting things pile up is a sure way to put on the pressure. When you learn to make the schedule your servant, you will no longer be its slave.

ACCENTUATE THE POSITIVE, ELIMINATE THE NEGATIVE

I like to think of every task I have to do as an opportunity. After I have established my priorities, eliminated illegitimate demands on my time, scheduled my day, and committed every moment to the Lord, I know of a certainty that each task, even an unexpected one, is an opportunity to grow, achieve, and succeed. Every second of my day and every task written in my schedule is an opportunity from the Lord; and I set about doing them with joy and confidence, because I'm certain God will put me over. No matter what pressures each day may bring, I face the day with the knowledge that I have the victory in Jesus Christ.

Look at *your* tasks as opportunities. You will have

a fresh new outlook every day when you look forward to the things you are privileged to do. Remember, each day holds the potential of blessing, achievement, victory, and overcoming. Stay in an attitude of praise toward the Lord for every opportunity He puts in your path. God wants you to give Him the opportunity to bless you and make you a blessing. When pressure arises, take the opportunity to put God in the midst of it and to demonstrate to yourself and others that you are an overcomer and the devil is a loser.

Several years ago a very popular song was entitled, "Accentuate the Positive, Eliminate the Negative." I like that advice! At all times and in every situation, it is so important to do just that, accentuate the positive and eliminate the negative. It is especially important when you are under pressure. Don't stay under pressure; get on top of it with a healthy attitude. A positive outlook and healthy attitude will be yours when you accentuate the positives of God's Word.

You must ignore negative counsel and stick to the promises in the Word of God. Never listen to voices of unbelief, fear, discouragement, and frustration even when the voice belongs to a well-meaning person. That person may be a friend, or that person may even be *you*. But always keep in mind that Satan is the one prompting all the negative thoughts. The devil is your *real* enemy, not yourself, your friends, your enemies, and certainly not the Lord.

Hope in God, because He is your best friend, the source and resource of all you need. There is no pressure too great to defeat you when you focus on the Lord instead of focusing on yourself and those things which put pressure on you and your time. Turn the tables around by putting pressure on the pressure. I often recall that King David, the wonderful psalmist, continually encouraged his own soul by accentuating the positive and eliminating the negative. May I encourage you to do the same? You'll soon find yourself outside the pressure cooker:

Why art thou cast down, O my soul? and why art thou disquieted within me? hope thou in God: for I shall yet praise him, who is the health of my countenance, and my God (Psalms 42:11).

O bless our God, ye people, and make the voice of his praise to be heard: Which holdeth our soul in life, and suffereth not our feet to be moved (Psalms 66:8,9).

CHAPTER SIX
Sowing and Reaping

GOD ESTABLISHED THE PRINCIPLE OF SOWING AND REAPING

While the earth remaineth, seedtime and harvest, and cold and heat, and summer and winter, and day and night shall not cease (Genesis 8:22).

From Genesis to Revelation the Bible continually speaks about the law of sowing and reaping. This is the basic principle upon which we must act to produce *anything* and *everything* in our lives. God's Word imparts this truth to us in a myriad of ways and examples because God earnestly desires that we know how to make our lives productive. Unless "seed" is first sown, no future harvest will be reaped. There is always an investment required before a gain is ever made. A seed is an investment in the future; plant good seed, and you will reap a good future.

Our God, Who wisely designed and set in motion the law of sowing and reaping, obeyed His own law by planting His Seed in the earth. That Seed was the Lord Jesus Christ, the most valuable and fruitful Seed that ever existed. God made this costly investment to reap a priceless harvest. Just as a farmer today sows seed expecting to produce a crop, God sowed His Seed expecting to reap a bountiful harvest more precious to Him than any other thing in all His vast universe:

And I [God] *will put enmity between thee* [Satan] *and the woman, and between thy seed and her seed* [Jesus], *it shall bruise thy head, and thou shalt bruise his heel* (Genesis 3:15).

Did God get results after sowing His Seed? Just look around you. The harvest which God expected is now measured in redeemed human lives like yours and mine, lives brought back into union and communion with God. Every believer has been recreated in the image and likeness of God's Seed, because seed always produces after its own kind. Now, because we are like Christ, we can have the fellowship with God which He so greatly desires; and when we obey God's principle of sowing and reaping, we too will produce results.

If God the Father had not sown His divine, yet human, Seed in the earth and had not let It die, then It would have remained alone and there would never have been a harvest of souls in the earth. Just think of it—that single Seed, which has been producing for centuries, is still producing Its harvest and will continue to do so until the season of harvest is over. We have no greater example of sowing and reaping than this One given to us by God:

And Jesus answered them, saying, The hour is come, that the Son of man should be glorified. Verily, verily, I say unto you, except a corn [seed] *of wheat fall into the ground and die, it abideth alone: but if it die, it bringeth forth much fruit* (John 12:23,24).

116

In spite of the vast harvest of people God has reaped from His Seed, this would all have been impossible if God had not found one man who would sow *his* seed. That man was Abraham and the "seed" which he was willing to sow was his own son Isaac, the son of promise whose miraculous birth Abraham and Sarah had awaited 25 years. Because of Abraham's faith, God entered into a covenant relationship with Abraham which required mutual giving and receiving.

God desired to give Abraham an abundance of spiritual and material blessings through a covenant agreement between them. God was willing to give His presence and His blessing to Abraham if Abraham was willing to give everything he had to God. Therefore, if God was to give His Son, Abraham had to give his son. God had promised the covenant would be fulfilled through Isaac, so Abraham was willing to sacrifice Isaac, believing that God would raise him from the dead. What courageous faith:

> *. . . By myself have I sworn, saith the LORD, for because thou hast done this thing, and hast not withheld thy son, thine only son: That in blessing I will bless thee, and in multiplying I will multiply thy seed as the stars of the heaven, and as the sand which is upon the sea shore; and thy seed shall possess the gate of his enemies; And in thy seed shall all the nations of the earth be blessed; because thou hast obeyed my voice* (Genesis 22:16-18).

Now to Abraham and his seed were the promises made. He saith not, And to seeds, as of many; but as of one, And to thy seed, which is Christ (Galatians 3:16).

GOD'S WORD IS SEED

Just as Jesus is God's Seed, so also the *Word* of God is His Seed. The beloved apostle John wrote:

In the beginning was the Word, and the Word was with God, and the Word was God. And the Word was made flesh, and dwelt among us, (and we beheld his glory, the glory as of the only begotten of the Father,) full of grace and truth (John 1:1,14).

Jesus, the Seed, is the unique Word of God; but *every* word of promise that has proceeded from God is also "seed" which will never fail to produce a harvest when it is sown by faith:

For as the rain cometh down, and the snow from heaven, and returneth not thither, but watereth the earth, and maketh it bring forth and bud, that it may give seed to the sower, and bread to the eater: So shall my word be that goeth forth out of my mouth: it shall not return unto me void, but it shall accomplish that which I please, and it shall prosper in the thing whereto I send it (Isaiah 55:10,11).

Jesus Himself illustrated through the "parable of the sower" that His Word is seed to be planted

(Matthew 13:18-23; Mark 4:3-20; Luke 8:5-15). In the parable a sower went out to sow his seeds. Some seed fell by the wayside and was eaten by birds; some seed fell on stony ground and soon sprouted, but the sun scorched the little plants because there was no deep soil for roots. Still other seed fell among thorns which choked out the plants. However, some of the seed fell on good ground and yielded a harvest in varying degrees, some thirty, some sixty, and some a hundred times.

When Jesus explained the parable to his disciples, He told them the *Word of God* is the "seed" sown into people's hearts by the Sower Who is the Son of God (Matthew 13:37). Although Satan could steal some of the Word from people before they understood it, the Word did not produce in other lives because these people did not hold fast to the Word when affliction, persecution, cares, riches, and lust pressed upon them.

Nevertheless, those who heard the Word with understanding and faith were able to stand against every difficulty and onslaught by using the very Word which the enemy tried to steal from them. These "Word people" were able to produce good fruit in their lives. After the Word was sown into their hearts, these people of faith sowed the Word into the difficulties and opportunities of their lives and reaped harvests in different measures.

I believe those who sowed the Word successfully 30 percent of the time reaped a 30 percent harvest, but unfortunately that is a 70 percent crop failure. Even those who brought forth a 60 percent harvest suffered a 40 percent loss. However, those who consistently sowed the Word into every situation reaped the hundredfold harvest. I don't like crop failures, and I don't think the Lord does either. Jesus tells us in this parable that we can be successful in every endeavor—100 percent of the time—if we always sow the good seed of the Word and wait patiently for the harvest which it will inevitably produce:

But that on the good ground are they, which in an honest and good heart, having heard the word, keep it, and bring forth fruit with patience (Luke 8:15).

Did you know that the Word says every believer is also God's seed? God has entrusted to His children the task of sowing His Word in the world and multiplying themselves. Just as the seed of God's Word reproduced Christ in me, I can also sow the Word into others and see the likeness of Christ reproduced in them. It thrills me to think that God has planted you and me in the earth to bring forth a good harvest for Him. Not only do I have the privilege of reaping success and achievement for myself but I also have the opportunity to sow the Word into other lives and reap those souls for the kingdom of God. I can think of no better way to spend my time:

The field is the world; the good seed are the children of the kingdom; . . . (Matthew 13:38).

120

EACH MOMENT OF TIME IS A SEED TO SOW

We don't have anything that has not been given to us by our gracious and loving heavenly Father. It is He who puts into our hands everything we need, and it is He Who supplies all the "seed" we need to sow in order to reap our harvest. Not only has the Lord promised seed to His children but He also promises the increase from that seed. However, seed must be sown before it will produce and multiply; otherwise, it remains just as it is:

> *And God is able to make all grace abound toward you: that ye, always having all sufficiency in all things, may abound to every good work: Now he that ministereth seed to the sower both minister bread for your food, and multiply your seed sown, and increase the fruits of your righteousness* (II Corinthians 9:8,10).

When we think of all the blessings the Lord has given to us in the *natural* realm, what is the foundational blessing upon which our entire life is built? I would have to say that gift is time. God placed mankind in the dimension of time; and as I said before, our very existence is measured in moments of time. Each minute is a "seed gift" from the Lord which each and every individual must sow wisely and thoughtfully if anything is to be gained. When we sow the minutes of our days profitably, we will maximize our days God's way.

Time which is wisely invested will inevitably reap a harvest of success, achievement, and satisfaction. However, time which is foolishly sown to the wind will bring forth nothing but emptiness. When a person continually discards, ignores, or wastes those precious seeds of time, that person's life will eventually become a waste, a field full of weeds instead of a field full of abundant and good produce. Life and time are too precious to waste!

The scripture says in Ecclesiastes 3:1 that *"To every thing there is a season, and a **time** to every purpose under heaven."* Paul the apostle told Timothy to be *instant* in season and out of season (see II Timothy 4:2). Paul is telling his young son in the faith to *stand firm* and *remain the same* in whatever circumstance or "season of time" he may find himself. This is implied by the Greek word *ephistemi* which is translated "instant" in II Timothy.

The prefix *ephi* means "to superimpose" or "to place something over or into something else." Paul instructed Timothy to *superimpose* the Lord into all circumstances and seasons. By standing firm in his faith and on the Word of God without wavering, Timothy would reap godly results. When we, like Timothy, "plant" God and His Word into the "ground" of our circumstances, that Word will produce! The Word has the power to move and change the situation for the better whether it is a "good" season or a "bad" season.

We have all had those seasons when, after having

sown our time and having done all we know to do, nothing seems to be turning out right. It may *appear* that all we have is a crop of weeds. That is the time to "hang on," keep sowing the seed of God's Word, and patiently wait for the harvest. I'm so thankful that the Holy Spirit has given us numerous accounts in the Bible of other people who succeeded when they superimposed the Word over a situation by applying God's principles. Abraham's son, Isaac, found himself in just such a situation; but sowing in faith produced dramatic results for him.

During a season of great famine in the land of Canaan, Isaac went into the area of Gerar which was inhabited by the Philistines. It appeared that Isaac wanted to go down to Egypt to escape the famine. However, God instructed Isaac not to go there but to spend the time in Gerar. It was in this alien place and at this difficult time that the Lord renewed and repeated to Isaac the covenant promise which He had made to Abraham. God was telling Isaac that if he would believe the promise, then Isaac would succeed and not fail in spite of famine or any other difficulty.

I'm happy to say that Isaac trusted the Lord and took the time to plant his seed even though there was no evidence that it would produce a crop. I can just hear the taunts and jeers of Isaac's neighbors, "Don't be a fool, Isaac! Why are you wasting good time and good seed by planting during a drought and famine? Don't you know you are wasting time planting seed which will never produce? You might as well eat the seed. At least you won't die of starvation today."

Isaac wouldn't have gone hungry that day, but what about the next day—and the next? Isaac chose to believe God's Word:

> *Then Isaac **sowed** in that land, and **received** in the same year an hundredfold: and the LORD blessed him. And the man waxed great, and went forward, and grew until he became very great* (Genesis 26:12,13).

The Bible continues Isaac's story by telling us that God blessed Isaac with great possessions of herds, flocks, and servants. Eventually the Philistines became envious of Isaac.

Isn't that just like people in the world today? They are quick to discourage and give negative advice; but when believers spend time sowing good seed into any and every situation and come out blessed, these people are jealous of God's blessing. The world tells us we had better hang on to what little we have or we will have nothing. However, the Word tells us to sow or give what we have, especially when it is little, so God can bring an increase—and what an increase God can bring! Isaac received a hundredfold. I'd rather do things God's way, wouldn't you?

GOD GIVES VARIETIES OF SEED

Thus far, several different kinds of "seed" have been mentioned: Jesus the Seed, the Word of God, God's children who are also the seed of Abraham by faith (see Galatians 3:29), and that very important seed—time. However, there are many other kinds of "seed." If the farmer wants several kinds of crops, then he must sow several different kinds of seed. What other seeds can we sow that will yield a bountiful harvest?

We all have a variety of seeds to sow including talent, money, training, experience, and position. Your very life is a seed to sow. What about sowing the "fruit of the spirit": love, joy, peace, longsuffering, gentleness, goodness, faith, meekness, and temperance? (See Galatians 5:22,23.) We can all sow friendship, a smile, a touch, a word of encouragement, a listening ear, and understanding. Or what about prayer? What marvelous seeds to sow to reap harvests of answers! I dare say most of us have more "seeds" in our "pockets" than we have ever counted. Let's take them out and plant them.

Do you remember what God said to Moses when Moses protested about becoming God's deliverer for Israel? Moses thought he had no talent for the job—he was 80 years old, he couldn't speak well, he had tried once and failed, not to mention that he was wanted in Egypt for murder! Did God listen to Moses? No! God said, "Moses what's that in your hand?" "Why God," replied Moses "that's just a stick, my shepherd's staff." But that staff was just enough. It was the seed Moses had to plant for a great harvest.

God, Moses, and that staff delivered Israel out of the hands of the cruel Egyptians. When Moses trusted and obeyed, the Lord enabled him to turn the river Nile into blood, bring every manner of plague upon Egypt, part the Red Sea—and deliver over four million Israelites. May I ask what it is that *you* have in *your* hand? Whatever it is may look to you like just an old stick; but if you will sow it unto God, He and you and that "old stick" will reap a bountiful and good harvest.

The soil in which we plant our seed is also very important. There are many kinds of good soil that will enable your seed to produce an abundant harvest. I would say that first of all you must take the time to sow God's Word into your heart. Only then can you effectively sow the Word into your life. Plant the good seeds of love and care into your family and loved ones. The harvest of love which you will receive in return is worth every moment of your time.

Sow your time, talent, energy, prayer, and money into the kingdom of God. The Word tells us that if we put His kingdom first in our lives, then we will reap everything we rightly desire in our life (see Matthew 6:33). That sowing begins with your local church, but you can reap harvests around the world when you plant seeds into the mission field. You don't have to sow just in your own backyard; there is a worldwide harvest of souls to be reaped. Sow the precious seeds you have into the lives of others whether those lives are in your own home, next door, or around the globe:

. . . behold, I [Jesus] say unto you, Lift up your eyes, and look on the fields; for they are white already to harvest. And he that reapeth receiveth wages, and gathereth fruit unto life eternal: that both he that soweth and he that reapeth may rejoice together (John 4:35,36).

SOWING IS LIKE GIVING

Perhaps you have already realized that sowing is much like giving. A seed must be sown or "given away" before it can multiply and produce a crop for the farmer. For a season the farmer has given his seed to the ground. In like manner we can consider some portion of everything we have as seed which must be given away before it can reproduce for us. God tells us it is more blessed to give than to receive. In this context the word *blessed* actually implies that it is more productive to give than to receive. Proverbs 11:24 says, *"There is that scattereth, and yet increaseth; and there is that withholdeth more than is meet, but it tendeth to poverty."*

When people spend their time on selfish pursuits and think only of what they can gain for themselves, they will lose what they have. However, those persons with generous hearts who spend some amount of their time and energy giving away or sowing a portion of what God has given to them will reap bountifully in this life and in the life to come. God loves a cheerful giver, and God will see to it that what is given will be multiplied back to the giver. A person who gives is a wonderful reflection of God to the world, and the blessings which come to a giver will stimulate others to seek the Lord:

> *And he* [Jesus] *said unto them, Take heed what ye hear: with what measure ye mete, it shall be measured to you: and unto you that hear shall more be given. For he that hath, to him shall be given: and he that hath not, from him shall be taken even that which he hath* (Mark 4:24,25).

God's principles are infallible; just as the seed must be sown and die in order to produce and multiply a harvest of life, so some of our "seed" must be "sown" in order for us to receive an abundance. What we possess must be given away before it is multiplied. If we hoard our seed rather than sow it, then there will certainly be no increase. Instead, we will lose what we do have. While these truths are contrary to the human mind, every farmer who has ever planted seed knows that they work; and every individual who has given has received in some way more than he has given:

> *Give, and it shall be given unto you; good measure, pressed down, and shaken together, and running over, shall men give into your bosom. For with the same measure that ye mete withal it shall be measured to you again* (Luke 6:38).

Please notice these scriptures in Mark and Luke not only tell us about the increase, they also describe the proportion of increase. If a farmer sows only a few seeds into a small plot of ground, he will have a small harvest, but if he sows many seeds over a wide area he will reap a bumper crop. Whatever amount you and I sow, we will receive according to that portion which we have sown. Each of us has the privilege of determining what kind of measure we will receive. If you sow a cupful, you will reap in cupfuls; but if you sow in basketfuls, your return will be in basketfuls:

But this I say, He which soweth sparingly shall reap also sparingly; and he which soweth bountifully shall reap also bountifully (II Corinthians 9:6).

Up to this point, I have mentioned only good seed and good soil; but unfortunately, there is always the possibility of planting bad seed or planting in bad soil. No farmer in his right mind would plant seed which he knew would not produce a good crop nor would he plant in soil which he knew to be unproductive. However, most of us along life's pathway have reaped a few weeds or a bad crop. Some of us right now may need to pray for a crop failure because we've sown some bad seed or planted in the wrong soil.

God's Word tells us about some of the bad seeds we can sow and some of the poor crops we can harvest. For examples, read Proverbs 6:14,19; 11:18; 16:28; 22:8. The Lord cautions us, as it were, to read the labels on our seed packets. Our heavenly Father has carefully labeled the packets of sin and iniquity for our protection. He loves each of us so very much that He warns us about the kinds of crops we can produce when we sow bad seed. Nevertheless, we all have a choice to make.

If an individual sows discord, hatred, strife, or jealousy, then that is what will be reaped. If a person sows gossip, slander, and judgment, then they open themselves to judgment and loss of reputation. There is neither time nor space here to list all the varieties of sin, but most of us know what they are. Consider very carefully what kinds of seed you are planting because, if you plant sin, you will not reap righteousness any more than you will grow tomatoes if you plant squash. It just doesn't work that way:

> *For they have sown the wind, and they shall reap the whirlwind: it hath no stalk: the bud shall yield no meal: if so be it yield, the strangers shall swallow it up* (Hosea 8:7).

> *Be not deceived; God is not mocked: for whatsoever a man soweth, that shall he also reap. For he that soweth to his flesh shall of the flesh reap corruption; but he that soweth to the Spirit shall of the Spirit reap life everlasting. And let us not be weary in well doing; for in due season we shall reap, if we faint not* (Galatians 6:7-9).

WAIT PATIENTLY FOR
THE HARVEST

Another important factor in sowing and reaping is the time *between* the sowing and the reaping. There certainly is a time to plant and a time to harvest. No gardener would plant lettuce seeds today and expect to pick lettuce tomorrow. Neither can you expect to plant today and reap a harvest tomorrow. Some crops do have a short growing season, but many others do not. Patience and endurance are required before our "crops" come to maturity and we begin to reap the benefit.

I will never forget the spring my husband Wally put out tomato plants and I interfered. Thinking Wally had put the plants in a poor spot, I dug them up and replanted them in a different location. A few weeks later, I decided on a "better" place for our tomato plants so I dug them up again and put them in the new spot. Wally warned me that I was hindering our tomato crop rather than helping it because the plants could not establish a good root system. But, of course, I thought I knew better. Meanwhile visions of big, ripe tomatoes danced in my head; but when it was time to pick the tomatoes, they were still only a vision. My impatience had ruined our crop.

The crops in our lives take time to grow and produce. Achievement and success in any area do not happen overnight. If we become impatient and give up, then we will never see the reward of our planting.

I know a woman who had a strong desire to become an accomplished pianist. Sally didn't have the opportunity to take piano lessons as a child, and she exhibited little evidence of talent. Nevertheless, after she was married and had a family, Sally started taking piano lessons; she began to sow seed for her harvest.

Weeks, months, and even years went by while Sally diligently continued at the piano. Her pursuit required more than just desire; Sally's training required a teachable spirit, careful adherence to instruction, and hours of time spent in practice. Accomplishment also required Sally's willingness to play for others even when the fear of failing was almost overwhelming. Many times Sally's playing fell far short of what was desired, but she was persistent enough to keep on trying. Sally even enrolled in college to earn a music degree.

Now, *years* later, Sally has become the accomplished musician she always wanted to be—but not without effort and a confidence that the Lord would enable her to achieve her goal. Sally is always willing to share her talent, and she has a genuine compassion to train young and old alike who wish to play the piano. Today Sally has a thriving music studio with as many as 30 students, and she is also the pianist in her church. This woman finds great reward in praising the Lord with her skill and seeing her students begin to accomplish their goals in music. Sally didn't reap her harvest in a short period of time; it took years of effort. But she earnestly and patiently waited for the fruit of her labor, and now she is enjoying that fruit.

TEND YOUR HARVEST

None of us has to know exactly how God is working out the details of our affairs to bring in our harvest after we have sown our seed; we only have to be diligent in doing our part and patient enough to wait for the reward. Does the farmer know and understand the process by which a seed becomes a plant and then produces fruit? Is that knowledge a requirement before there is a harvest from the seed? Of course not. If it were, then there would never be a crop of any kind. The farmer only needs to tend to the planting, watering, fertilizing, and weeding; the life in the seed will do the rest.

When we sow into our goals and into the lives of others, God will make a way for us to reap our harvest even when there is no way. When there is no resource, God is always our Source. The Lord can provide finances when there seems to be no means of supply; He can open doors for us that seem forever shut. God is able to put us in the right place at the right time and give us opportunities we could never imagine. God has the power to make the impossible possible when we trust Him and do our part. If we sow, we shall certainly reap:

And he [Jesus] *said, So is the kingdom of God, as if a man should cast seed into the*

> *ground; And should sleep, and rise night*
> *and day, and the seed should spring and*
> *grow up, he knoweth not how. For the earth*
> *bringeth forth fruit of herself; first the blade,*
> *then the ear, after that the full corn in the*
> *ear. But when the fruit is brought forth,*
> *immediately he putteth in the sickle,*
> *because the harvest is come* (Mark 4:26-29).

Some amateur gardeners think that *all* they must do to have an abundant harvest is to plant seed and let the garden take care of itself. Unfortunately, that is not true. The man of whom Jesus spoke in the previous scripture did more than sleep and rise. Although he was not worried about how the seeds would produce the plants, he cared and tended to his crop with the assurance that if he did his part, the seed would do its part. Whenever necessary that man weeded, hoed, and watered his prospective crop. Without that kind of attention, the crop would have failed.

Have you ever seen a would-be garden, in the middle of the summer, which is overgrown with weeds and the ground is parched for lack of water? Probably some ambitious person got off to a good start in the spring but failed to tend and care for the garden. Perhaps the "gardener" either didn't plan garden care into the schedule or just got lazy and decided it wasn't worth the trouble. Whatever the reason, that person will have nothing to harvest; and the effort which was put into the garden was wasted.

Any harvest we intend to reap in our lives must be well tended. It isn't enough to have visions and plans. It isn't even enough to make schedules or to be enthusiastic at the onset of a project. There is work to be done. We need to have absolute confidence in the Lord to move in supernatural ways on our behalf, but we also must do our part to keep the "soil" in good condition. There is some "weeding, hoeing, and watering" to be done. It is the industrious and diligent Christian who reaps abundant harvests.

It is my great desire for you to sow all your good seed into the soil of projects and activities which will produce bountiful harvests. Never forget that each day is a precious seed, a promise of success and accomplishment. Don't waste your seeds. Sow them into good things and good places, and you will have no regrets in the many seasons of harvest. Maximize your day God's way, and you will be a fruitful tree in God's garden of life!

Chapter Seven
From Here to Eternity

"Only one life, 'twill soon be past . . . "

Although you cannot find this well-known quote in the pages of scripture, there is a sobering truth in these words which certainly agrees with the infallible truth of God's Word. Fortunately, this quote concludes with a most positive and encouraging thought: " . . . Only what's done for Christ will last." How absolutely true! There is only one way to transfer anything from here to eternity, and that way is to do everything for the glory of the Lord:

Whether therefore ye eat, or drink, or whatsoever ye do, do all to the glory of God (I Corinthians 10:31).

Most of us have also heard the old adage, "There are no pockets in a shroud," which grimly restates the fact that, "You can't take it with you." Certainly there are no pockets in a burial robe; and in all human existence, none have ever been needed. No one has ever, nor will ever, take any of this *world's* goods with him into the next life. Nevertheless, many individuals have attempted to do just this; the towering pyramids of Egypt are just one example. Lives and lifetimes were spent building these massive tombs, but there was no future in them.

On several occasions my husband Wally and I have gazed upon the ancient pyramid tombs of the Pharaohs and seen the sarcophagi which contain the mummified remains of those whose images are carved on these ornate caskets. I am always grieved by the evidence that the ancient Egyptians centered their "way of life" around entering the next life with all their earthly goods. Of course, it was all to no avail. Centuries later when these tombs were opened, they still contained every article placed within them— including the corrupted remains of their owners. What a sad commentary on a society that was ignorant of God's eternal ways!

In recent years certain individuals have had their bodies frozen after death hoping that modern technology would eventually find a way both to revive them and sustain life forever. What an impossible effort for those who struggle to hang on to this *present* life. Although this may be a very ingenious idea, it is nevertheless futile. These souls have escaped their bodies' icy entombment to face immediately the endless life they had hoped for— without Christ. What a shock awaited these persons when they stepped into the hereafter! How tragic! They didn't know that God had made a way into a glorious eternity through His Son Jesus—and they missed it.

I find that the longer I live, the more I am aware of the eternal nature of my spirit and soul. Obviously, the Lord has placed an innate sense in every human being that we are destined for eternity. Humanity fights death and struggles to live—forever. There is a strong desire in each of us that cries out to know and find union with a supreme, eternal deity. Every culture and religion in the world incorporates some ideology concerning a continuing existence after physical death as well as some idea of an eternal God.

This life just isn't long enough to fulfill all the visions and dreams that excite human imagination; it isn't long enough to sustain all the gifts and talents that could be expressed through any individual. If Beethoven were alive today, I know he would still be writing symphonies. If Rembrandt were living, he would still be painting. The apostle Paul said that *"If in this life only we have hope in Christ, we are of all men most miserable"* (I Corinthians 15:19). Paul looked forward to eternity, even longed to step over into that realm of existence where he would enjoy the full revelation of God and himself.

We as Christians know that the Lord never intended for life to be thwarted and cut short by death; but through Adam and Eve, sin poisoned all humanity and brought forth physical and spiritual death. Nevertheless, God provided a Way to bridge the gap from here to eternity through the vicarious death of His divine Son, Jesus:

> *For God so loved the world, that he gave his only begotten Son, that whosoever believeth in him should not perish, but have everlasting life* (John 3:16).

Because this is true, how do we prepare for eternity and a life that will last forever? It isn't enough just to put our efforts into things that will fade with the passing of time. Jesus Himself told us not to store up our treasures on earth where they are subject to destruction, but that we should and could lay up treasures in heaven where they would never be destroyed. The greatest treasure anyone possesses is one's soul; therefore every person first of all needs to accept Jesus as Savior and Lord. This is the only way to ensure eternity spent with God and not without Him. However, if all your treasure is on earth, you will have little interest in heaven:

Lay not up for yourselves treasure upon earth, where moth and rust doth corrupt, and where thieves break through and steal: But lay up for yourselves treasures in heaven, where neither moth nor rust doth corrupt, and where thieves do not break through nor steal; For where your treasure is, there will your heart be also (Matthew 6:19-21).

Whatever we accomplish in this life is done within the framework of time, and Jesus made it clear that what we do with our time will count for eternity. In other words, the effects of what we do with every precious moment will go on forever. This is a very sobering fact, and it should cause each of us to examine carefully what we are doing with our time. Is it going to count on the positive side of our record or is it going to count on the negative side? Are you wasting time in fruitless pursuits or are you "buying up" your time in productive endeavors that will precede you into heaven? Just how important is it to you to maximize your days God's way?

I have mentioned people of the past and the present who made elaborate but fruitless plans for life after death. On the other hand, Jesus spoke of a man who lived his days and planned his *earthly* future as though he would *never* have to face eternity. This near-sighted man was so caught up in this *present* life that he gave no thought to a *future* life. The abundant harvest which his land had produced caused this rich farmer to plan on building bigger and better barns to hoard his increase. He spent his time thinking of ways to lay up all his treasure on earth:

> *And he said, This will I do: I will pull down my barns, and build greater; and there will I bestow all my fruits and my goods. And I will say to my soul, Soul, thou hast much goods laid up for many years; take thine ease, eat, drink, and be merry* (Luke 12:18,19).

This greedy man gave no thought to the possibility of sharing his increase with people less fortunate than himself. The man's covetous heart thought only of the life of ease his bounty would secure for him. Never in the time he spent sowing and reaping had he ever planned for the moment when he must face the "grim reaper" of death. And yet, even while he gloated over what his abundance would provide, God interrupted his reverie with words that dashed all his hopes to the ground—words that instantly terminated all plans for his earthly future:

> But God said unto him, Thou fool, **this** night
> thy soul shall be required of thee: then whose
> shall those things be, which thou hast
> provided? (Luke 12:20).

Jesus concluded the parable by speaking a profound thought intended for each of us, *"So is he that layeth up treasure for himself, and is not rich toward God"* (Luke 12:21). The Bible is full of illustrations and examples of men and women, even boys and girls, who have made a choice, a choice for either death or life. Some have chosen an earthly life of self-gratification only to receive eternal death in the end, but many have chosen death to self in this life in order to enjoy eternal life with God:

> . . . I [God] have set before you life and death,
> blessing and cursing: therefore choose life,
> that both thou and thy seed may live:
> That thou mayest love the LORD thy God,
> and that thou mayest obey his voice, and
> that thou mayest cleave unto him: for he
> is thy life, and the length of thy days; . . .
> (Deuteronomy 30:19,20).

How utterly foolish it is to spend time trying to get what you cannot keep in exchange for what you cannot lose. That is certainly not the way to maximize your day God's way! When we get the most and the best out of every moment of our day His way, we have not only succeeded in life that day but we have succeeded in setting aside a reward for an eternal "day":

He that findeth his life shall lose it: and he that loseth his life for my [Jesus'] *sake shall find it* (Matthew 10:39).

HAVE A HEAVENLY VIEWPOINT

Over and over the Scriptures contrast poorly spent lives with wisely spent lives. One of the Egyptian mummies in which I was particularly interested was that of the Pharaoh who is believed to have defied God and Moses, only to drown in the Red Sea. You must go to Egypt to see the remains of Ramses II (1301-1234 B.C.); however, you can ''see'' Moses—in the Word of God every day—standing with Jesus on the ''Mount of Transfiguration,'' fellowshiping with the Lord. The Pharaoh spent his lifetime amassing a fortune and an empire, while Moses spent most of his life ''laying up treasures in heaven'' by following and obeying God.

Do you realize that Moses had been groomed to be Egypt's next Pharaoh? Moses could have had the immediate gratification of this world's fame and fortune, but he chose instead to wait on God. At the age of 40, Moses fled the splendors of the Egyptian court because he took a stand for the Hebrew slaves. Moses spent the next 40 years tending sheep in a desert until God knew he was ready to spend an additional 40 years leading ''God's sheep'' through the wilderness. And where is Moses now? He is enjoying the *eternal* splendor of the courts of heaven.

143

Pharaoh refused to listen to God and left nothing to posterity, but Moses heard God's voice and left to Israel and the world a knowledge of the true and living God. It was Moses who wrote the first five books of the Bible:

By faith Moses, when he was come to years, refused to be called the son of Pharaoh's daughter; Choosing rather to suffer affliction with the people of God, than to enjoy the pleasures of sin for a season; Esteeming the reproach of Christ greater riches than the treasures in Egypt: for he had respect unto the recompense of the reward (Hebrews 11:24-26).

I don't know about others; but like Moses, I prefer the reward that awaits God's children who have laid up an abundance of treasure in heaven. I desire to spend my days and my hours doing those things that are profitable for eternity. Personally, I have chosen to send my treasure ahead of me into heaven rather than pile it up here on earth. The wonderful thing about living my life with a view of heaven is that my view of earth is so much better. I watch people who live only for self-gratification, and they are not really happy. But those who live to serve the Lord and others are the happiest people on earth—and I'm one of them. How about you?

Abraham, the father of our faith, was a man with a heavenly viewpoint and a love for God. Because Abraham kept his eyes on God and His Word, he received an abundance of this world's goods; but Abraham didn't serve the Lord just for the earthly blessing. Abraham loved God and preferred the heavenly reward more than the earthly reward. When this man from Chaldea heard God's call and left his home in Ur, it was with the knowledge that God was not only leading him to a land here on earth but also to an eternal dwelling place. Abraham was looking for an eternal city whose builder and maker is God:

> *By faith Abraham, when he was called to go out into a place which he should after receive for an inheritance, obeyed; and he went out, not knowing whither he went. For he looked for a city which hath foundations, whose builder and maker is God* (Hebrews 11:8,10).

SPEND YOUR DAYS BUILDING ON THE RIGHT FOUNDATION

God's Word speaks often about buildings and foundations. Isn't it fascinating that God chose to place His Son in the home of a carpenter? No doubt Jesus spent most of His earthly time building things—and He is still building today. Jesus told Peter that the revelation and acknowledgement of Jesus as the Son of God is the "rock" or foundation upon which He would build His Church (Matthew 16:15-18). Every person who confesses Jesus as Lord and Savior is fitted by the Lord into the building of His Church as a *living* stone. Jesus Himself is the chief cornerstone (Isaiah 28:16; I Peter 2:6):

> *Ye also, as lively stones, are built up a spiritual house, an holy priesthood, to offer up spiritual sacrifices, acceptable to God by Jesus Christ. Wherefore also it is contained in the scripture, Behold, I lay in Sion a chief corner stone, elect, precious: and he that believeth on him shall not be confounded* (I Peter 2:5,6).

In I Corinthians 3:9-11 the apostle Paul wrote about an eternal foundation which is laid right here on earth. Paul referred to himself as a wise master builder who, by preaching the gospel and winning souls for Christ, laid the foundation upon which God's living temple is built. Paul warned believers to be careful as to how they spent time constructing their lives upon the foundation of Jesus Christ. Unfortunately, some are going to enter eternity without rewards even though they attain heaven through faith in Jesus. These people will never have found time to make Jesus *Lord* nor time to live for Him.

Two kinds of people are compared by Paul—those who spend their days profitably with eternity in view and those who spend their days unprofitably for only temporal and momentary satisfaction. Christians who work to build fruitful and selfless lives are building on the foundation of Christ with *imperishable* things that Paul compared to gold, silver, and precious stone. Neither time nor eternity will destroy their labor. However, Christians who spend selfish lives in fruitless effort are building with *perishable* material such as wood, hay, and stubble, which is here today but gone tomorrow:

> *Now if any man build upon this foundation gold, silver, precious stones, wood, hay, stubble;* **Every man's work shall be made manifest**: *for the day shall declare it, because it shall be revealed by fire: and the fire shall try every man's work of what sort it is. If any man's work abide which he hath built thereupon, he shall receive a reward. If any man's work shall be burned, he shall suffer loss: but he himself shall be saved; yet so as by fire. Know ye not that ye are the temple of God, and that the Spirit of God dwelleth in you?* (I Corinthians 3:12-16).

Is there any question that what we do now counts for eternity? It is only while we are *here in the dimension of time* that any of us have the time or opportunity to accept Christ, to live for His glory, and to labor for Him and His kingdom. Then we will enjoy true personal success. This very day, which you are living now, will count for eternity one way or the other. If your time is spent in a truly profitable way which complies with God's Word, it will produce a heavenly profit with an eternal reward. Time well spent pays good dividends. On the other hand if you waste your life in idleness or selfish ambition, you will see your reward go up in smoke. I'm certain you want more than ashes to present to the Lord Jesus:

> *I beseech you therefore, brethren, by the mercies of God, that ye present your bodies a living sacrifice, holy, acceptable unto God, which is your reasonable service. And be not conformed to this world: but be ye transformed by the renewing of your mind, that ye may prove what is that good, and acceptable, and perfect, will of God* (Romans 12:1,2).

I remember so well the days when there were "hippies" on our streets. These confused young men and women protested the materialism of our modern society, but they had no answers for either here or eternity. Spiritually empty, they wasted their bodies on drugs and their lives in aimless wandering. I also remember how the young people of our church went out into the streets—to witness of the love and life-changing power of Jesus. Many of the "hippies" who heard the "good news" accepted Jesus as Savior and Lord.

Soon the front rows of our sanctuary were filled with young men and women who didn't look at all like the average churchgoer. Their hair was long and stringy, their clothing was shabby, and they were sometimes barefoot; but as a congregation we reached out to these precious souls. Without our "preaching" to them or saying a word about their lifestyle or appearance, the Holy Spirit and the

Word of God began to change them. Each one found a purpose for living and a direction for life, which included eternity.

Let me tell you what has happened to two or three of the young men who had been wasting their days until Jesus came and changed their lives. Two of them married fine Christian women whom they met in the church. In fact, one of the men married one of the girls who had witnessed to him on the street. This young man cleaned up his act, started a business, and today he and his wife have a lovely family and are living for the Lord. The wife certainly invested her time wisely for her future, don't you think?

One member of our "group" now has his doctorate in theology and is teaching youngsters in a private school, where he is given the freedom to teach the Word of God and its eternal principles. He also heads the Christian education department of the church he and his wife attend. Another of the young men received a Bible college education and is now laboring for Christ in a large church in Africa. The young women who came out of that destructive lifestyle have also received hope and direction for their lives. I could tell you about many more of these "treasures" who are living lives of achievement and success today. The direction and purpose of each life was eternally changed by a small group of young people who took the time to share Jesus—time that will count for eternity!

USE ALL YOUR TIME PRODUCTIVELY

How casually and carelessly time is often spent without any consideration for the fact that we will each give an account to God for the way we invest our time. Time is a lot like money; it can be wasted in foolish pursuits, or it can be invested wisely so that it brings future dividends. I like the way Paul begins his letter to the church in Thessalonica, and I have great admiration for those believers to whom Paul could say:

> *We give thanks to God always for you all, making mention of you in our prayers; Remembering without ceasing your* **work of faith**, *and* **labour of love**, *and* **patience of hope** *in our Lord Jesus Christ,* **in the sight of God and our Father;** *knowing brethren beloved, your election of God* (I Thessalonians 1:2-4).

What are those things mentioned in the 13th chapter of I Corinthians that will abide forever? Of course, they are faith, hope, and charity. These are the nature and character of God, and they cannot pass away. After the demonstration of many fine deeds have faded and been forgotten, we are told that any demonstration of true faith or hope or godly love will last forever. I'm sure the Holy Spirit also includes any word or action that inspires faith, hope, or love in another individual. When all is said and done, only those achievements and successes we have

150

accomplished through faith, hope, or love will last through eternity.

Difficult circumstances and trials of every sort are often blamed for lack of achievement and are used as excuses for wasting time. Nevertheless, it is possible to triumph in the most difficult of times and circumstances. The list of those courageous people who have conquered every sort of circumstance is endless, and names are being added to the list every day. These people have lived not only for the "here and now" but they also have lived for eternity. God's Word encourages us with many such examples.

One midnight, long ago, two badly beaten men sat chained in a dark, dirty, stinking Philippian prison; but they were neither complaining nor wringing their hands. Nor did they bemoan the fact that their fine work of evangelism had been stopped by the unjust accusations of those who had put them in jail. On the contrary, Paul and Silas were singing praises to God! Although their prayer and praise service did not arouse their nearby jailer, it did get the attention of Almighty God in heaven.

The next thing that jailer knew, the earth was shaking violently and he saw to his dismay that the doors to the inner prison were open. Supposing the prisoners had escaped, the jailer drew his sword to kill himself rather than be executed by his superiors. However, Paul called to the jailer and told him no one had left the prison. The Philippian jailer was smart enough to recognize divine intervention when he saw it, and he cried to Paul and Silas for salvation.

Because there was never a day, *or a night*, when Paul and Silas lost sight of their eternal destiny, they could be optimistic in the worst situation. Through praise and worship, these two men redeemed time which otherwise would have been lost and, thereby, gave the Lord opportunity to turn an evil situation into something good. Consequently, the Lord gave Paul and Silas opportunity to lead the jailer and his entire family to Jesus. Paul and Silas found time to show this family the way from "here to eternity." I've often wondered if it were not this Philippian jailer whom Paul saw in the vision that called him to Macedonia.

Paul was not unaccustomed to jails or imprisonment. The last years of Paul's life were spent in prison or under house arrest. Although he was *physically* unable to reach the world with the gospel during this time, Paul reached more people by the wise use of those days than he did at any other period of his life. Paul did this by writing letters to the young churches scattered around the world. Most of these churches Paul had started himself. Today those letters are still bearing fruit since Paul's epistles comprise much of the New Testament. What a loss it would have been if Paul had not had the time to write those letters because he was too busy traveling and preaching the gospel.

The beloved apostle John wrote the book of Revelation in his "spare time" when he was exiled on the Isle of Patmos after years of ministry to the Body of Christ. Imagine the loss the Church would have suffered if John had not received that wonderful revelation of heaven and our glorious and triumphant Lord. How ignorant we would be of "end times" if John had not picked up a pen to write his revelation. I'm so thankful we can read the "last page" of the Book and see the glorious outcome of the Church. Isn't it great to know the devil loses and **we win**:

> *And what shall I more say? for the time would fail me to tell of Gedeon, and of Barak, and of Samson, and of Jephthae, of David also, and Samuel, and of the prophets: Women received their dead raised to life again: and others were tortured, not accepting deliverance; that they might obtain a better resurrection: And these all, having obtained a good report through faith, received not the promise: God having provided some better thing for us,* **that they without us should not be made perfect** (Hebrews 11:32,35,39,40).

TIME WELL SPENT BRINGS AN ETERNAL REWARD

There is coming a day when all of us will stand together before Christ and give an account of those things which we have done while we were here on earth. How we spend our days is so important to the Lord that He is keeping a record of every one of them. Jesus wants to *reward* us for the Christlike activities which occupied the days allotted to us in this earthly life. Isn't that wonderful? However, if you have been careless or selfish with the precious days the Lord has given to you, this information may bring a twinge of conviction to your heart. If you are not satisfied with the way you have been spending the moments that tick away your life, it is not too late to change. *Decide right now* to start maximizing each day God's way:

> *For none of us liveth to himself, and no man dieth to himself. For whether we live, we live unto the Lord; and whether we die, we die unto the Lord: whether we live therefore, or die, we are the Lord's. So then every one of us shall give account of himself to God* (Romans 14:7,8,12).
>
> *Wherefore we labour, that, whether present or absent, we may be accepted of him. For we must all appear before the judgment seat of Christ; that every one may receive the things done in his body, according to that he hath done, whether it be good or bad* (II Corinthians 5:9,10).

We all want to know that our life's work has been productive. Life seems hopeless and futile unless we have achieved some measure of success in the areas to which we have applied ourselves. The reward of our effort may be immediate, such as the pleasure expressed by a family when Mom has prepared a delicious meal. The reward may come later, such as a diploma earned after four years of hard work in college. The reward may be a simple, "Thank you," after driving a neighbor to the doctor; or it may be the long-lasting satisfaction we enjoy in the success and maturity of our children after we have put everything we had into training and raising them.

Whether the reward for our time and effort here is momentary or long-lasting, God sees it all. When we have put forth our best effort because His love has prompted us, the Lord has a reward for us that will last throughout eternity. Even the smallest act of kindness will ultimately bring eternal reward. Sometimes we work diligently at something and no one seems to notice or maybe our effort seems to be taken for granted, but we know and God knows. A satisfied heart from a day well spent or a task well done is often the best reward.

The great successes and accomplishments that catch the world's attention do not necessarily impress the Lord. Although He desires that we all achieve to our fullest potential, God is impressed with our motives. He sees right to the heart of every matter— your heart and my heart. Selfish ambition will never count for much with the Lord, and the person who seeks *first* the acclaim of people will be disappointed when heavenly rewards are given. Jesus has told us to live each day and do each task for God and not

for the applause of others (see Matthew 6:1-18).
*Take heed that ye do not your alms before
men, to be seen of them: otherwise ye have
no reward of your Father which is in
heaven. Therefore when thou doest thine
alms, do not sound a trumpet before thee, as
the hypocrites do . . . that they may have
glory of men. Verily I say unto you, They
have their reward. But when thou doest
alms, let not thy left hand know what thy
right hand doeth: That thine alms may be
in secret: and thy Father which seeth in
secret himself shall reward thee openly*
(Matthew 6:1-4).

When I was a little girl, I was fascinated with stories of gorgeously gowned princesses with glittering crowns on their heads, who lived in the majestic splendor of faraway castles. Those were just stories in books for children, but God's Book tells a true story of something far better and more real awaiting His children. We will live in heavenly mansions which Jesus is preparing for us (see John 14:2), and we will be clothed in shining white robes (see Revelation 7:9). The Lord will crown us with life (see James 1:12; Revelation 2:10), righteousness (see II Timothy 4:8), and glory (see I Peter 5:4). Some people spend their days on earth striving for corruptible crowns, but God's saints live so as to receive incorruptible crowns:
*And every man that striveth for the mastery
is temperate in all things. Now they do it to*

obtain a corruptible crown; but we an incorruptible (I Corinthians 9:25).

Such expectation thrills me, but the thing that thrills me most is the thought of seeing Jesus face-to-face and hearing Him say, "*. . . Well done, thou good and faithful servant: thou hast been faithful over a few things, I will make thee ruler over many things: enter thou into the joy of thy lord*" (Matthew 25:21). Those who have overcome in this life will rule with Christ throughout eternity. I am convinced that the overcomers are those who have ruled in this life one day at a time, conquering the obstacles, difficulties, trials, and challenges with determination and the *help of God*:

Cast not away therefore your confidence, which hath great recompence of reward. For ye have need of patience, that, after ye have done the will of God, ye might receive the promise. For yet a little while, and he that shall come will come, and will not tarry (Hebrews 10:35-37).

"*. . . only what's done for Christ will last.*"

Receive Jesus Christ as Lord and Savior of Your Life.

The Bible says, *"That if thou shalt confess with thy mouth the Lord Jesus, and shalt believe in thine heart that God hath raised him from the dead, thou shalt be saved. For with the heart man believeth unto righteousness; and with the mouth confession is made unto salvation"* (Romans 10:9,10).

To receive Jesus Christ as Lord and Savior of your life, sincerely pray this prayer from your heart:

Dear Jesus,

I believe that You died for me and that You rose again on the third day. I confess to You that I am a sinner and that I need Your love and forgiveness. Come into my life, forgive my sins, and give me eternal life. I confess You now as my Lord. Thank You for my salvation!

Signed _____

Date _____

Write to us.

We will send you information to help you with your new life in Christ.

Marilyn Hickey Ministries • P.O. Box 17340
Denver, CO 80217 • (303) 770-0400

For Your Information
Free Monthly Magazine

☐ Please send me your free monthly magazine
OUTPOURING (including daily devotionals,
timely articles, and ministry updates)!

Tapes and Books

☐ Please send me Marilyn's latest product catalog.

Mr. & Mrs.
Miss
Mrs.   Please print.
Name Mr _____

Address _____

City _____

State _____ Zip _____

Phone (H) (   ) _____

(W) (   ) _____

Mail to
Marilyn Hickey Ministries
P.O. Box 17340
Denver, CO 80217
(303) 770-0400

Prayer Request(s)

Let us join our faith with yours for your prayer needs. Fill out the coupon below and send to Marilyn Hickey Ministries, P.O. Box 17340, Denver, CO 80217.

Prayer Request(s) _____

_____

_____

_____

_____

_____

Mr. & Mrs.   Please print.
Mr.
Name Miss _____
     Mrs.

Address _____

City _____

State _____ Zip _____

Phone(H) (   ) _____

         (W) (   ) _____

If you want prayer immediately, call our Prayer Center at
(303) 796-1333, Monday-Friday, 4 a.m. - 4:30 p.m. (MT).

WORD
to the
WORLD
COLLEGE

Explore your options and increase your knowledge of the Word at this unique college of higher learning for men and women of faith. Word to the World College offers **on-campus and correspondence courses** that give you the opportunity to learn from Marilyn Hickey and other great Bible scholars. WWC can help prepare you to be an effective minister of the gospel. Classes are open to both full- and part-time students.

For more information, complete the coupon below and send it to:

Word to the World College
P.O. Box 17340
Denver, CO 80217
(303) 770-0400

Mr.   Please print.
Mrs.
Name Miss _____

Address_____

City _____ State _____ Zip _____

Phone (H) _____ (W) _____

BOOKS BY MARILYN HICKEY

A Cry for Miracles ($7.95)
Acts of the Holy Spirit ($7.95)
Angels All Around ($7.95)
Armageddon ($4.95)
Ask Marilyn ($9.95)
Be Healed ($9.95)
Bible Can Change You (The) ($12.95)
Bible Encounter Classic Edition ($24.95)
Book of Revelation Comic Book (The) ($3.00)
Break the Generation Curse ($7.95)
Daily Devotional ($7.95)
Dear Marilyn ($7.95)
Devils, Demons, and Deliverance ($9.95)
Divorce Is Not the Answer ($7.95)
Especially for Today's Woman ($14.95)
Freedom From Bondages ($7.95)
Gift-Wrapped Fruit ($2.95)
God's Covenant for Your Family ($7.95)
God's Rx for a Hurting Heart ($4.95)
Hebrew Honey ($14.95)
How to Be a Mature Christian ($7.95)
Know Your Ministry ($4.95)
Maximize Your Day...God's Way ($7.95)
Names of God (The) ($7.95)
Nehemiah—Rebuilding the Broken Places in Your Life ($7.95)
Next Generation Blessings (The) ($9.95)
No. 1 Key to Success—Meditation (The) ($4.95)
Release the Power of the Blood Covenant ($4.95)
Satan-Proof Your Home ($7.95)
Save the Family Promise Book ($14.95)
Signs in the Heavens ($7.95)
What Every Person Wants to Know About Prayer ($4.95)
When Only a Miracle Will Do ($4.95)
Your Miracle Source ($4.95)
Your Total Health Handbook— Body • Soul • Spirit ($9.95)

MINI-BOOKS: $1⁰⁰ each
by Marilyn Hickey

Beat Tension
Bold Men Win
Bulldog Faith
Change Your Life
Children Who Hit the Mark
Conquering Setbacks
Don't Park Here
Experience Long Life
Fasting and Prayer
God's Benefit: Healing
God's Seven Keys To Make You Rich
Hold On To Your Dream
How To Become More Than a Conqueror
How To Win Friends
I Can Be Born Again and Spirit Filled
I Can Dare To Be an Achiever
Keys to Healing Rejection
Power of Forgiveness (The)
Power of the Blood (The)
Receiving Resurrection Power
Renew Your Mind
Solving Life's Problems
Speak the Word
Standing in the Gap
Story of Esther (The)
Tithes • Offerings • Alms • God's Plan for Blessing You
Turning Point
Winning Over Weight
Women of the Word

Covering the Earth with His Word!

You are my Faith Covenant Partner and I want you to know what we are doing in the ministry. It was over 20 years ago that God showed me He would bring men and women together (like an army) to carry out His mission to "cover the earth with the Word." He reminded me that He would not only anoint and bless the ministry, He also declared that He would anoint and bless each partner as we shared the vision and the victory.

As my Faith Covenant Partner, you are helping me not only to fulfill the call of God on my life, but you are literally helping to impact nations for Christ as we, together, carry the light of the gospel into the uttermost parts of the world. Truly, the words of Isaiah are being fulfilled in our midst: "... the earth shall be full of the knowledge of the LORD, as the waters cover the sea" (Isaiah 11:9). *Marilyn*

One of the few women ever to preach in Pakistan in an open, public forum, Marilyn and her ministry team pioneered new but dangerous territory as they proclaimed the gospel during a Miracle Healing Crusade and Ministry Training School in Lahore.

MHM joined forces with relief agencies in war-torn Bosnia and Rwanda to provide emergency food, medical supplies, clothing, hygiene items, and Bibles.

MHM contributed to the ongoing outreach of the Mission of Mercy which feeds two meals a day to approximately 15,000 street people in Calcutta, India, and over 20,000 people daily in Cambodia and Vietnam.

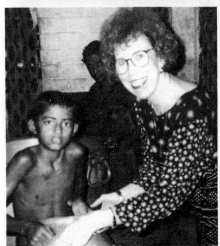

There was joy like a river in Hungary during Marilyn's recent speaking engagement. The crowds were ecstatic as the Holy Spirit descended upon them, setting them free to weep, rejoice, and be healed and delivered in the mighty name of Jesus.

Marilyn and her international ministry team stormed hell's gates in Russia and Ukraine during Marilyn's miracle ministry cruises to both countries and a crusade in Ukraine.

Over 800 children have been permanently affected by the gospel of Jesus Christ through MHM's support of evangelization, administrative work, and the expansion of classroom space in the only two Christian schools located in the mountains of Honduras.

In addition to
leading ministry
teams into China to
take Bibles and other
Christian literature,
MHM supports a
Chinese church and
pastor who distribute
thousands of Bibles
each month; a tract
distribution ministry;
Chinese couriers
who deliver Bibles
and teaching
materials; and
several Chinese
orphanages.

Marilyn has ministered in Ethiopia on
several occasions, and is being used of
God to establish a continuing program of
Bible and food distribution to the people
in this war-torn land.

Marilyn Hickey
Ministries' worldwide
crusades are
impacting nations for
the gospel of Christ
as she travels
throughout the world
proclaiming Jesus as
Lord.